slow cooking
curry & spice
dishes

slow cooking
curry & spice
dishes

carolyn humphries

foulsham
LONDON • NEW YORK • TORONTO • SYDNEY

foulsham

The Oriel, Thames Valley Court, 183-187 Bath Road,
Slough, Berkshire SL1 4AA, England

Foulsham books can be found in all good bookshops and direct from
www.foulsham.com

ISBN 978–0–572–03406–1

Cover photograph © The Anthony Blake Picture Library

A CIP record for this book is available from the British Library

The moral right of the author has been asserted

Other books for your slow cooker:
Slow Cooking from Around the World (978–0–572–03289–0)
New Recipes for Your Slo-cooker (978–0–572–02636–3)
Real Food from Your Slo-cooker (978–0–572–02536–6)
Slow Cooking for Yourself (978–0–572–03150-3)
Slow Cooking from Around the Mediterranean (978–0–572–03323–1)
Slow Cooking for Vegetarians (978–0–572–03387–3)

Printed in Great Britain by CPI Mackays, Chatham ME5 8TD

CONTENTS

INTRODUCTION

Curries, in particular, have become *the* new-age food, popular with young and old alike. We owe it to the spice routes, which started as long ago as 2000 BC, for bringing the sweet warmth and fire of exotic Eastern spices to Western shores; but I think we should also thank the migration of peoples from all parts of the globe for bringing us the diversity of taste and texture that you get from curries and other spicy dishes.

But now you don't have to rely on take-aways or restaurants to give you those authentic meals. Using your slow cooker means you can come home to a perfect dish, gently simmering in the pot ready for you to serve with rice or accompany with warm breads. Others can be cooked in just an hour or two for when you don't want to wait all day. The slow cooking renders the dishes meltingly tender and also helps those exotic flavours to develop to their full potential. Plus the slow cooker uses only about as much fuel as a light bulb, so it's much better than having a pot simmering on the stove or in the oven.

This book is packed with a whole range of curry and spicy dishes from Thailand to China, South America to Africa – and there's even the occasional British speciality to tickle the taste buds. The added bonus with all the recipes is that, as there is only a little added fat and salt, unlike many take-aways, they are extremely good for you.

USING YOUR SLOW COOKER

1 Stand the electric base on a level, heat-resistant surface. Do not use on the floor.

2 Do not preheat your pot unless your manufacturer's instructions tell you to.

3 Put the ingredients in the ceramic crock pot, then put the pot in the base.

4 Add boiling liquid.

5 Cover with the lid and select the cooking temperature – High, Medium (if you have it) or Low. Note that some smaller cookers cook quite quickly on High so you may find that cooking on the Low setting is preferable, particularly if you are not going to be there to keep an eye on things or are cooking only a smallish quantity. And, if you will be out all day, choose the Low setting.

6 Cook for the recommended time. If there is a range of time, check after the shorter time given; this will usually be sufficient for most cookers but the food won't spoil for the extra time.

7 Taste, stir and re-season, if necessary.

8 Switch off the cooker and remove the crock pot using oven gloves.

COOKING TIPS FOR USING THE SLOW COOKER

- Any of your usual curry and chilli recipes can be cooked in your slow cooker but remember that liquid doesn't evaporate as much as it does when cooking conventionally, so cut down the liquid content by 30–50 per cent. You can always add a little extra liquid at the end of cooking, if necessary.
- Should there be too much liquid at the end of cooking, strain it into a saucepan and boil rapidly for several minutes until it is reduced to the quantity and consistency you require. Alternatively, you can thicken it with a little flour or cornflour blended with a little water, or a little extra creamed coconut, if appropriate.
- If wanting a brown finish to meat or poultry, fry it quickly in a frying pan before adding to the crock pot.
- For many dishes, it is best to quickly fry onions before adding them – the flavour is completely different from slow cooking them from raw.
- Make sure all frozen foods are thawed before use.
- Cut root vegetables into small, even-sized pieces and put them towards the bottom of the pot as they take longer than meat or other vegetables to cook.
- Do not cook too large a joint or bird in the crock pot. It should fit in the pot with at least a 2.5 cm/1 in headspace. If unsure, cut the joint or bird in half before cooking (it will then cook quicker, as when cooking conventionally).
- Dried beans must always be boiled rapidly in a saucepan of water for at least 10 minutes before adding them to your crock pot, to destroy toxins.
- If preparing food the night before you wish to start cooking, store the ingredients in the fridge overnight. Put them in the crock pot in the morning and cover with boiling liquid or sauce before cooking.

- Do not open the lid unnecessarily during cooking as heat will be lost. If you remove it to add extra ingredients or to stir more than once or twice, you may need to add an extra 10 minutes at the end (but in most cases there is sufficient cooking time allowed in the recipes for this).
- When food is cooked the cooker can be switched off and left for up to 30 minutes. The food will stay piping hot. If you need to leave food keeping hot for longer, switch to Low (this isn't suitable for egg-based or rice dishes).
- Most foods can be cooked on High or Low (or Medium or Auto-cook if you have these). Fish, rice and egg-based dishes, however, should always be cooked on Low.
- If you are planning on being out all day, opt for cooking on Low, then there is little or no chance of the meal ruining even if you are back later than you had planned (particularly if you don't have a programmable slow cooker).
- Use a crock pot suitable for the quantity of food you want to cook. It should be at least a third to half full for best results, though for foods that are bathed in a sticky glaze, such as spicy buffalo wings, a single layer in a large pot is fine. Don't use a small pot and pack it in tightly to the top or the heat won't be able to penetrate the food – just as when cooking conventionally. But, conversely, don't have too small a quantity either. For instance, one chop in the pot will overcook unless the pot is filled up to at least a third with liquid. So, if cooking for one, you may need to double the amount of liquid to be on the safe side.

LOOKING AFTER YOUR SLOW COOKER

- Do not put the crock pot or the lid in the oven, freezer or microwave or on the hob or under the grill (broiler).
- Do not plunge the hot pot into cold water after cooking or it may crack.
- Do not leave the whole pot soaking in water as the base is unglazed and porous so will absorb the water. You may, however, leave water *in* the pot to soak it before washing.
- Do not preheat the cooker before adding the ingredients (unless your manufacturer's instructions tell you to).
- Do not use the slow cooker to reheat food.
- Do not leave uncooked food in the slow cooker when it is not switched on (so never put it in there overnight ready to switch on in the morning; store the ingredients in the fridge).
- Do not use abrasive cleaners on the crock pot – but it will be dishwasher-safe.
- Do not immerse the electric base in water; simply unplug it and wipe it clean with a damp cloth.

COOKING TIMES

Some crock pots now have three settings but others have only two. I have cooked all the foods in this book on High or Low as they will be relevant to all. If you use Medium, it will take a time mid-way between the times I have given in the recipes.

Some cookers also have Auto-cook. Follow your manufacturer's guidelines to use it. I recommend you use Low if you are going to be out all day. Cooking on High is great if you want quicker meals but don't cook small quantities or they will burn.

This chart also shows you the approximate conversion times from conventionally cooked dishes, should you want to try your own recipes (but remember to reduce the liquid by at least a third). Always check your manufacturer's instructions too as the times may vary slightly.

Please note, when cooking fish, rice and eggs you should always use Low for best results.

The more you use your slow cooker, the more you will become used to the correct times for your own model.

Conventional cooking time	Slow cooking time in hours		
	High	Medium	Low
15–30 minutes	1–2	2–3	4–6
30 minutes–1 hour	2–3	3–4	5–7
1–2 hours	3–4	4–6	6–8
2–4 hours	4–6	6–8	8–12

NOTES ON THE RECIPES

- I designed these recipes, for the most part, to be cooked in a large oval 6.5 litre slow cooker but many can be cooked in a smaller, round 3.5 litre cooker. Remember that some small models cook quite quickly on High, so you may prefer to use the Low setting.
- All ingredients are given in imperial, metric and American measures. Follow one set only in a recipe. American terms are given in brackets.
- The ingredients are listed in the order in which they are used in the recipe.
- All spoon measures are level: 1 tsp=5 ml; 1 tbsp=15 ml.
- Eggs are medium unless otherwise stated.
- Always wash, peel, core and seed, if necessary, any fresh produce before use.
- Seasoning is very much a matter of personal taste. Taste the food before serving and adjust to suit your own palate.
- There is a whole range of chillies available. I haven't called for loads of different ones – just fat and thin. You can experiment with the ones you like best. In general, the large, fat ones are milder than thin, finger ones. In all of them, most of the fire is in the seeds and white pith so, for delicate palates, remove these before use.
- Don't buy dried spices in large quantities unless you cook with them all the time. They need to be stored in a cool, dark place and should be used within 6 months or the flavour will start to deteriorate.
- When I call for stock, use fresh if possible, or make up the equivalent with stock cubes or powder.
- I have called for stalks of lemon grass but you can substitute ready-crushed in a jar, using 5 ml/1 tsp per stalk. The same goes for fresh root ginger. In both cases the flavour won't be quite as good but they are a useful alternative. Store the jars in the fridge once opened.
- The can and packet sizes given are approximate as they vary from brand to brand.

POULTRY
DISHES

Although all varieties of poultry don't take long to cook conventionally, the meat can often be dry or stringy if overcooked, which is easily done. Using a slow cooker makes this almost an impossibility and produces moist, melting poultry curries and the best ever spicy buffalo wings! In this section, I've mostly used chicken but there are a few turkey and duck recipes for you to try too.

Chicken tikka masala – *a British invention and not Indian at all! – is usually marinated, then grilled, then stewed in sauce. Here, all the cooking is in the slow cooker; otherwise, by the time you've marinated and grilled before the main cooking, there'd be little point in using the slow cooker! The result tastes great, even if it may not be strictly 'authentic'.*

Non-grilled chicken tikka masala

SERVES 4

1 small sprig of fresh mint
1 onion, quartered
1 large garlic clove, halved
1 cm/½ in piece of fresh root ginger, peeled and roughly chopped
1 fat green chilli, seeded, if preferred, and roughly chopped
Juice of 1 lime
30 ml/2 tbsp tomato purée (paste)
15 ml/1 tbsp paprika
2.5 ml/½ tsp ground coriander
2.5 ml/½ tsp ground cumin
2.5 ml/½ tsp ground turmeric

5 ml/1 tsp garam masala
5 ml/1 tsp salt
15 ml/1 tbsp sunflower oil
200 ml/7 fl oz/scant 1 cup thick, creamy plain yoghurt
700 g/1½ lb skinless chicken breast, cut into bite-sized pieces
30 ml/2 tbsp ground almonds
30 ml/2 tbsp double (heavy) cream
Wedges of lime to garnish

TO SERVE:
Pilau rice or naan bread

1 Strip the mint leaves off the central stalk. Pound the mint, onion, garlic, ginger and chilli using a pestle and mortar or in a bowl with the end of a rolling pin to form a rough paste. Alternatively, use a hand blender.

2 Add the lime juice, tomato purée, all the ground spices and the salt. Mix together until well blended.

3 Heat the oil in a pan, add the paste and fry for 1 minute. Stir in the yoghurt and bring to the boil.

4 Put the chicken in the crock pot and pour the sauce over. Stir well. Cover and cook on High for 3 hours or Low for 6 hours.

5 Stir in the ground almonds and cream. Taste and re-season, if necessary. Garnish with wedges of lime and serve with pilau rice or naan bread.

For murghi bhuna masala *the chicken is usually first fried completely in a small amount of spicy sauce before stewing and the result is quite a dry curry. Here I've used similar spices to create a slow-cooked version that has more sauce and succulence. I like to scrape out the seeds from the cardamom pods to get the full flavour without the husks.*

Sautéed chicken in spice sauce

SERVES 4

30 ml/2 tbsp groundnut (peanut) or sunflower oil
25 g/1 oz/2 tbsp ghee or butter
4 chicken breasts with skin on, cubed or left whole
2 fat green chillies, seeded, if preferred, and chopped
2 large onions, finely chopped
1 large garlic clove, crushed
2 cardamom pods, split
1.5 ml/¼ tsp ground cloves

5 ml/1 tsp ground ginger
2.5 ml/½ tsp ground turmeric
400 g/14 oz/1 large can of chopped tomatoes
Salt and freshly ground black pepper
30 ml/2 tbsp chopped fresh coriander (cilantro)

TO SERVE:
Plain rice, raita (see page 107) and mango chutney

1 Heat the oil and ghee or butter in a frying pan. Add the chicken and brown quickly all over. Transfer to the crock pot.

2 Add the chillies, onions and garlic to the pan and fry, stirring, for 2 minutes.

3 Scrape the cardamom seeds into the onions and add all the remaining ingredients except the coriander. Bring to the boil. Tip into the crock pot, cover and cook on High for 2–3 hours or Low for 4–6 hours.

4 Taste and re-season, if necessary. Spoon over rice, sprinkle with the chopped coriander and serve with raita and mango chutney.

This is a version of poona murghi. *You can use a ready-roasted bird if you like, in which case just slow cook it for 1 hour on High. That way, it makes a great after-work dish instead of an all-day one. You can buy packets of ready-flavoured pilau rice, which are very acceptable. I like to serve a large mixed salad with it, too, to add texture and colour.*

Creamy spiced chicken

SERVES 4

30 ml/2 tbsp groundnut (peanut) oil
1 small chicken, about 1.5 kg/3 lb, quartered
1 large garlic clove, finely chopped
2.5 cm/1 in piece of fresh root ginger, finely chopped
5 ml/1 tsp paprika
5 ml/1 tsp ground turmeric
1.5 ml/¼ tsp hot chilli powder

2.5 ml/½ tsp salt
300 ml/½ pt/1¼ cups double (heavy) cream
30 ml/2 tbsp cornflour (cornstarch)
30 ml/2 tbsp water

TO SERVE:
Pilau rice

1 Heat the oil in a frying pan, add the chicken and brown all over. Transfer the chicken to the crock pot with a draining spoon and spoon off the excess fat from the pan.

2 Add all the remaining ingredients to the pan except the cornflour and water and bring to the boil, stirring. Pour over the chicken. Cover and cook on High 2–3 hours or Low for 4–6 hours until tender.

3 Blend the cornflour with the water and stir into the sauce. Cover and cook for a further 15 minutes until thickened.

4 Taste and re-season, if necessary. Serve with pilau rice.

Slow cooking the chicken in the spicy yoghurt means you don't need to marinate it first (though you can leave it in the fridge overnight if you want to), and the flavours penetrate as it cooks. The meat won't have the blackened-in-places look you might associate with a genuine tandoor-cooked dish, but it will have all the flavour and more succulence.

Tandoori chicken

SERVES 4–6

6 large chicken portions, halved
200 ml/7 fl oz/scant 1 cup plain
   yoghurt
Juice of 1 lime
1 garlic clove, crushed
2.5 ml/½ tsp ground ginger
2.5 ml/½ tsp ground cumin
30 ml/2 tbsp paprika

15 ml/1 tbsp garam masala
1.5 ml/¼ tsp hot chilli powder
A good pinch of salt
Wedges of lime to garnish

TO SERVE:
Plain rice, mango chutney and a
   mixed side salad

1   Pull off as much skin as possible from the chicken. Make several slashes in the thick parts of the flesh. Place in the crock pot.

2   Mix together all the remaining ingredients and spoon over the chicken. Rub the mixture well into the slits and turn the pieces over so they are coated completely.

3   Cover and cook on High for 2–3 hours or Low for 4–6 hours until the chicken is tender.

4   Lift the chicken out of the liquid with a draining spoon. Transfer to plates, garnish with wedges of lime and serve with rice, mango chutney and a mixed side salad.

You could make your own green curry paste, but the bought versions are very good. This recipe uses chicken, but it is also a rich and delicious dish when made with duck (you'll find a red duck curry on page 22). If you do try it with duck, make sure you let the dish stand for about 10 minutes after cooking, then you can easily spoon off the excess fat before serving.

Thai green chicken curry

SERVES 4

1 bunch of spring onions (scallions)
45 ml/3 tbsp sunflower oil
1 small chicken, about 1.25 kg/
    2½ lb, cut into 8 pieces
    (or 4 chicken portions, halved)
60 ml/4 tbsp Thai green curry paste
1 green (bell) pepper, diced
400 g/14 oz/1 large can of coconut
    milk

1 stalk of lemon grass, finely
    chopped
2 kaffir lime leaves
15 ml/1 tbsp Thai fish sauce
Salt and freshly ground black pepper

TO SERVE:
Egg noodles

1   Trim the spring onions. Finely chop one and reserve for garnish and cut the rest into short lengths.

2   Heat the oil in a frying pan, add the chicken and brown on all sides. Transfer to the crock pot.

3   Add the spring onions and curry paste to the pan and fry, stirring, for 1 minute. Add all the remaining ingredients, bring to the boil and pour over the chicken. Cover and cook on High for 2 hours or Low for 4 hours until really tender.

4   Taste and re-season, if necessary. Spoon over egg noodles and serve, garnished with the chopped spring onion.

This brightly coloured dish is one of my favourites. It's delicately exotic but very easy to prepare. Although not an authentic touch, I like to serve it piled on a bed of only-just-wilted spinach (pour boiling water over the leaves in a colander, toss, then drain well) as well as the rice, but you could also try lightly stir-fried pak choi, spring greens or Savoy cabbage.

Vietnamese yellow coconut chicken

SERVES 4

30 ml/2 tbsp groundnut (peanut) or sunflower oil
1 bunch of spring onions (scallions), finely chopped
2 garlic cloves, finely chopped
450 g/1 lb boned skinless chicken thighs or breasts, cut into pieces
10 ml/2 tsp ground turmeric
5 ml/1 tsp ground ginger
5 ml/1 tsp ground cumin
1 stalk of lemon grass, finely chopped

1–2 thin green chillies, seeded, if preferred, and finely chopped
100 g/4 oz creamed coconut
300 ml/½ pt/1¼ cups water
Salt and freshly ground black pepper
45 ml/3 tbsp single (light) cream
50 g/2 oz/½ cup roasted peanuts, chopped
A handful of torn fresh coriander (cilantro) leaves

TO SERVE:
Plain rice

1 Heat the oil in a pan, add the spring onions, garlic and chicken and fry, stirring, for 3 minutes. Tip into the crock pot.

2 Add all the spices to the pan with the coconut and water. Bring to the boil, stirring, until the coconut has melted. Tip over the chicken and season well.

3 Cover and cook on High for 2–3 hours or Low for 4–6 hours until tender and bathed in a rich sauce.

4 Stir in the cream, then taste and re-season if necessary. Serve over rice, sprinkled with the chopped roasted peanuts and torn coriander leaves.

Thai curries have really taken off in the last few years and their popularity shows no sign of waning. This version using duck instead of the more usual chicken is a wonderfully rich, succulent dish. It's important not to add any fat as there's plenty in the duck and to spoon off any residual fat before serving. Try serving it with a green salad with some green apple added.

Thai rich duck curry

SERVES 4

15 ml/1 tbsp groundnut (peanut) oil
1 oven-ready duck, about 2 kg/
  4½ lb, cut into 8 pieces
60 ml/4 tbsp Thai red curry paste
400 g/14 oz/1 large can of coconut
  milk
2 kaffir lime leaves
2 stalks of lemon grass, finely
  chopped

30 ml/2 tbsp Thai fish sauce
2 red (bell) peppers, cut into
  diamond shapes
Salt
8 torn fresh horapa or basil leaves

TO SERVE:
Jasmine rice

1 Heat the oil in a non-stick pan. Add the duck pieces and brown on all sides. Transfer to the crock pot with a draining spoon.

2 Stir the curry paste into the pan and cook, stirring, for 1 minute. Add the coconut milk, lime leaves, lemon grass and fish sauce. Bring to the boil, stirring, then pour over the duck.

3 Cover and cook on High for 3 hours or Low for 6 hours.

4 Add the pepper pieces and cook for a further 1 hour until the duck is meltingly tender. Add salt to taste. Scatter the horapa or basil leaves over and serve with jasmine rice.

This is a 'set' curry, unlike the more usual runny Thai recipes. You could try using chicken or pork instead of the turkey and substituting cabbage greens for the pak choi if that's more accessible. I don't recommend cooking this receipe on High as it might curdle so it's one to leave gently cooking on Low all day, ready to enjoy at the end of a busy working day.

Thai turkey curry with pak choi

SERVES 4

2–3 heads of pak choi, separated
   into leaves
2 eggs, beaten
400 g/14 oz/1 large can of coconut
   milk
15 ml/1 tbsp chopped fresh mint
15 ml/1 tbsp chopped fresh horapa
   or basil leaves
30 ml/2 tbsp Thai red curry paste
15 ml/1 tbsp Thai fish sauce

5 ml/1 tsp grated fresh root ginger
1 thin red chilli, seeded, if preferred,
   and finely chopped
1.5 ml/¼ tsp salt
450 g/1 lb turkey stir-fry meat
A few torn horapa or basil leaves
   to garnish

TO SERVE:
Jasmine rice

1 Blanch the pak choi leaves in boiling water for 2 minutes. Drain and use to line a 20 cm/8 in soufflé dish that will fit comfortably inside the crock pot (if using a small slow cooker, line the crock pot with the leaves).

2 Mix together the eggs, coconut milk, herbs, curry paste, fish sauce, ginger, chilli and salt.

3 Cut up any large pieces of meat, then mix into the egg mixture. Pour into the lined dish and cover with foil, twisting and folding under the rim to secure.

4 Place the dish in the crock pot and pour about 2.5 cm/1 in of boiling water around it. Cover and cook on Low for 6–8 hours until set and the turkey is tender.

5 Garnish with a few torn horapa or basil leaves and serve with jasmine rice.

This is a warming, comforting casserole for when you don't want to prepare much before you go out and want a meal ready when you get back. As it uses storecupboard ingredients, it makes a great standby meal that can be thrown together very quickly. Vary the flavour with celery or chicken soup instead of mushroom – but always use condensed.

English-style curried chicken casserole

SERVES 4

15 g/½ oz/1 tbsp butter
4 chicken portions
1 onion, chopped
2 celery sticks, chopped
100 g/4 oz button mushrooms, sliced
15 ml/1 tbsp curry powder

295 g/10½ oz/1 medium can of condensed mushroom soup
30 ml/2 tbsp chopped fresh parsley

TO SERVE:
Plain rice and a green salad including some fresh coriander (cilantro) leaves

1   Heat the butter in a frying pan, add the chicken and brown on all sides. Transfer to the crock pot with a draining spoon.

2   Add the onion, celery and mushrooms to the pan and fry, stirring, for 2 minutes until lightly golden. Stir in the curry powder and fry for 1 minute.

3   Stir in the can of soup, bring to the boil, stirring, and pour over the chicken. Cover and cook on High for 3 hours or Low for 6 hours until really tender.

4   Garnish with the chopped parsley and serve with rice and a fresh green salad.

When pumpkins aren't in season, use other orange-fleshed squashes such as butternut squash. If none are available, use sweet potatoes but make sure you cut them into quite small chunks as they may not cook quite so quickly as pumpkin. The sweetness of the vegetable blended with coconut and the slightly bitter green pepper is a wonderful combination.

Caribbean chicken and pumpkin curry

SERVES 4

60 ml/4 tbsp groundnut (peanut) or
   sunflower oil
700 g/1½ lb pumpkin, peeled,
   seeded and cut into bite-sized
   chunks
1 bunch of spring onions (scallions),
   chopped
1 garlic clove, crushed
5 ml/1 tsp ground turmeric
15 ml/1 tbsp curry powder
5 ml/1 tsp crushed dried chillies

90 ml/6 tbsp water
4 skinless chicken breasts, cubed
400 g/14 oz/1 large can of extra-
   thick coconut milk
Salt and freshly ground black pepper
1 green (bell) pepper, cut into
   diamond shapes
30 ml/2 tbsp toasted sesame seeds

TO SERVE:
Flat breads

1   Heat the oil in a large frying pan, add the pumpkin chunks and fry, stirring, for about 5 minutes until golden all over and almost tender. Remove with a draining spoon and drain on kitchen paper (paper towels). Set aside.

2   Reserve a few chopped green ends of spring onions for garnish. Add the remainder to the pan and stir-fry for 1 minute. Add the garlic, spices and water and stir for 30 seconds. Add the chicken and toss in the spice mixture, then tip into the crock pot.

3   Pour the coconut milk into the pan and heat, stirring, until bubbling. Add to the chicken, season with salt and pepper and mix well. Add the pumpkin and pepper diamonds, cover and cook on High for 2 hours or Low for 4 hours until the chicken and pumpkin are really tender.

4   Taste and re-season, if necessary. Sprinkle with the toasted sesame seeds and the reserved chopped green spring onion and serve with flat breads.

There are numerous versions of dhanzak *but this one is particularly good in the slow cooker. You can also make a prawn version; simply omit the chicken and substitute 400 g/14 oz of large raw, peeled prawns, thawed and dried if frozen, for just the last hour of cooking. Use two chillies, if you like a fiery curry, or increase the amount of chilli powder.*

Chicken and red lentil curry with tomatoes

SERVES 4

2 large potatoes, cut into walnut-sized chunks
4–6 skinless chicken breasts, cubed
175 g/6 oz/1 cup red lentils
15 ml/1 tbsp groundnut (peanut) or sunflower oil
1 onion, chopped
1 large garlic clove, crushed
1 fat green chilli, seeded, if preferred, and chopped
2.5 ml/½ tsp hot chilli powder
5 ml/1 tsp ground turmeric
10 ml/2 tsp ground cumin
5 ml/1 tsp ground coriander

1.5 ml/¼ tsp ground cloves
10 ml/2 tsp garam masala
750 ml/1¼ pts/3 cups boiling chicken stock
30 ml/2 tbsp malt vinegar
4 tomatoes, skinned and chopped
5 ml/1 tsp demerara sugar
Salt and freshly ground black pepper
30 ml/2 tbsp chopped fresh coriander (cilantro)

TO SERVE:
Plain rice

1   Put the potatoes, chicken and lentils in the crock pot. Stir well to mix everything together.

2   Heat the oil in a pan, add the onion and garlic and fry, stirring, for 1 minute. Stir in the chilli and dried spices and cook, stirring, for a further minute.

3   Add all the remaining ingredients except the chopped coriander, seasoning well. Bring back to the boil and pour into the pot. Stir, cover and cook on High for 3–4 hours or Low for 6–8 hours until everything is tender.

4   Taste and re-season if necessary. The sauce should be thick but not stodgy so thin it, if necessary, with a little boiling water. Serve garnished with the coriander with rice.

This is so easy and quick to put together and is delicious served with rice but I also like to serve it with stir-fried vegetables, flavoured with soy sauce and grated fresh root ginger. Use any selection of vegetables you have to hand, shredded or cut into matchsticks or thinly sliced. Alternatively, for speed, use a packet of ready-prepared stir-fry vegetables.

Simple Chinese chicken curry

SERVES 4

45 ml/3 tbsp groundnut (peanut) oil

2 onions, roughly chopped

3 garlic cloves, crushed

15 ml/1 tbsp curry powder

10 ml/2 tsp palm or light brown sugar

200 ml/7 fl oz/scant 1 cup chicken stock

Salt

30 ml/2 tbsp soy sauce

4 skinless chicken breasts, cut into chunks

45 ml/3 tbsp cornflour (cornstarch)

TO SERVE:

Plain rice

1 Heat the oil in a wok or frying pan, add the onions and garlic and fry, stirring, for 2 minutes. Stir in the curry powder and fry for a further 30 seconds. Add the sugar, stock and soy sauce, bring to the boil, taste and add salt, if necessary.

2 Toss the chicken in the cornflour and place in the crock pot. Add the boiling sauce, stir, cover and cook on High for 2–3 hours or Low for 4–6 hours until the chicken is really tender and the sauce is thick.

3 Taste and re-season if necessary. Serve spooned over rice.

This version of nasi bokhari *has a lovely rich flavour and colour. As this is a two-part recipe, I've given the option of cooking the rice on High to shorten the cooking time. It reheats remarkably well too, but use your microwave or a steamer, not the slow cooker. It's more time consuming than other recipes in this book but it's well worth the effort.*

Malaysian chicken with rice and almonds

SERVES 4

160 g/6 oz/1 small can of
  evaporated milk
30 ml/2 tbsp tomato purée (paste)
2 garlic cloves, crushed
Grated zest and juice of 1 lime
2.5 ml/½ tsp salt
5 ml/1 tsp ground cumin
5 ml/1 tsp ground coriander
5 ml/1 tsp ground turmeric
1 small piece of cinnamon stick
4 cardamom pods, split
2 star anise
5 ml/1 tsp grated fresh root ginger
25 g/1 oz/¼ cup ground almonds

1 small chicken, about 1 kg/2¼ lb,
  cut into 8 pieces and skinned
350 g/12 oz/1½ cups basmati rice
25 g/1 oz/2 tbsp ghee or butter
875 ml/1½ pts/3½ cups boiling
  chicken stock
A few torn fresh coriander (cilantro)
  leaves to garnish

FOR THE GARNISH:
15 ml/1 tbsp groundnut (peanut) oil
1 onion, halved and thinly sliced
30 ml/2 tbsp flaked (slivered)
  almonds
30 ml/2 tbsp raisins

1 Mix together the evaporated milk, tomato purée, garlic, lime zest and juice, the salt, all the spices and the ground almonds. Add the chicken, turn to coat well and leave to marinate for at least 3 hours or preferably overnight.

2 Wash the rice well in a sieve (strainer) and drain thoroughly.

3 Heat the ghee or butter in a frying pan. Lift the chicken out of the marinade, add to the pan and fry quickly on all sides to brown. Remove from the pan and place in the crock pot.

4 Add the marinade to the pan, bring to the boil, stirring, then pour over the chicken. Cover and cook on High for 2 hours or Low for 4 hours.

5 Lift out the chicken and set aside. Stir in the rice and boiling stock, then return the chicken on top, re-cover and cook on High for a further 45–60 minutes or Low for a further 1½–2 hours until the rice is cooked and has absorbed all the liquid and the chicken is meltingly tender.

6 Meanwhile, to make the garnish, heat the oil in a frying pan, add the onion and fry, stirring, until golden. Stir in the flaked almonds and raisins and fry for a further 1 minute. Drain on kitchen paper (paper towels).

7 When the dish is cooked, transfer the chicken to warm plates, fluff up the rice and add. Sprinkle with the onion mixture and scatter a few torn coriander leaves over.

Chicken wings cook really well in the slow cooker. If your barbecue is all fired up and ready to go, you could throw them on at the end to crisp and brown, if you like, though they are very moreish just moist and tender. You really need a large oval cooker for this so they are distributed evenly in the pot but you could cook half the quantity in a smaller crock pot.

Spicy buffalo wings

SERVES 4

16 chicken wings, about 1 kg/2¼ lbs
1 large garlic clove, crushed
30 ml/2 tbsp clear honey
5 ml/1 tsp made English mustard
90 ml/6 tbsp tomato ketchup
  (catsup)

60 ml/4 tbsp tomato purée (paste)
30 ml/2 tbsp red wine vinegar
30 ml/2 tbsp soy sauce
30 ml/2 tbsp Worcestershire sauce
5 ml/1 tsp hot chilli powder

1 Cut the tips off the chicken wings at the first joint and discard. Place the wings in the crock pot.

2 Mix together all the remaining ingredients in a large saucepan. Bring to the boil, add to the chicken and toss well, then spread the wings out evenly in the pot.

3 Cover and cook on High for 2–3 hours or Low for 4–6 hours until tender and coated in a rich sauce, rearranging the chicken once for best results.

This recipe is based on the many versions of this dish from the Caribbean and South America. It has a fiery sweet flavour and really does need no more than the plain potatoes (or perhaps rice) and avocado salad I suggest to offset it. If you want to tone down the heat a little, use only one chilli – though that could be said to defeat the object of the dish!

Chilli pepper pot

SERVES 4

4 chicken portions, each cut in half
450 g/1 lb belly pork (with the
   bones in)
1 large onion, chopped
2 thin red chillies, seeded, if
   preferred, and chopped
1 red (bell) pepper, diced
1 green pepper, diced
15 ml/1 tbsp dark brown sugar
2.5 ml/½ tsp ground cinnamon
A good pinch of ground cloves

2.5 ml/½ tsp dried thyme
10 ml/2 tsp red wine vinegar
5 ml/1 tsp tamarind pulp
300 ml/½ pt/1¼ cups boiling water
Salt and freshly ground black pepper
A few drops of Tabasco sauce, to
   taste (optional)

TO SERVE:
Plain boiled potatoes and an
   avocado salad

1 Put the chicken, pork, onion, chillies and peppers in the crock pot. Blend together all the remaining ingredients except the Tabasco, if using, seasoning with some salt and lots of pepper and pour over.

2 Cover and cook on High for 3 hours or Low for 6 hours until everything is tender.

3 Leave to stand for 10 minutes, then spoon off the excess fat. Taste and add a few drops of Tabasco, if liked. Serve hot with potatoes and an avocado salad.

The Aztec idea of adding cocoa or unsweetened chocolate to sauces gives them a wonderful depth of flavour! You'll also find a beef mole recipe that uses cocoa on page 48. Use chicken portions instead of breasts, if you prefer. For an authentic touch, serve the mole as the Mexicans do, with rolled-up flour tortillas to mop up the juices.

Chicken mole with baby corn

SERVES 4

30 ml/2 tbsp olive oil

4 chicken breasts (preferably with skin on)

100 g/4 oz baby corn cobs, cut into chunks

1 green (bell) pepper, diced

1 red pepper, diced

1 large onion, diced

1 large garlic clove, crushed

400 g/14 oz/1 large can of chopped tomatoes

15 ml/1 tbsp tomato purée (paste)

1–2 thin green chillies, seeded, if preferred, and chopped

15 g/½ oz dark (semi-sweet) chocolate with 70 per cent cocoa solids, finely grated

A few drops of Tabasco sauce, to taste (optional)

Salt and freshly ground black pepper

TO SERVE:

Plain rice and a mixed salad

1 Heat the oil in a frying pan, add the chicken and fry on all sides to brown. Place in the crock pot and add the corn.

2 Add the peppers and onion to the pan and fry, stirring, for 2 minutes. Add to the pot.

3 Add the garlic, tomatoes, tomato purée, chillies, chocolate and Tabasco, if using, to the pan and bring to the boil, stirring. Season to taste, then pour over the chicken. Cover and cook on High for 3 hours or Low for 6 hours until really tender.

4 Serve on a bed of rice with a mixed salad.

From North Africa, a tagine refers to the dish it is traditionally cooked in as well as the spiced meat and fruit casserole itself. There are numerous versions (of course!) but all of them lend themselves to slow cooking with very successful results. This one has the extra kick of some hot chilli powder and I particularly like the addition of almonds for texture.

Hot and sweet spiced chicken and apricot tagine

SERVES 4

4 chicken portions
1 small lemon, halved
25 g/1 oz/2 tbsp butter
2 onions, thinly sliced
1 green (bell) pepper, thinly sliced
5 ml/1 tsp ground cinnamon
1.5 ml/¼ tsp ground cloves
15 ml/1 tbsp harissa paste
2.5 ml/½ tsp dried oregano
100 g/4 oz/⅔ cup ready-to-eat stoned (pitted) apricots, halved

50 g/2 oz/½ cup blanched (slivered) almonds
30 ml/2 tbsp thick honey
300 ml/½ pt /1¼ cups boiling chicken stock
30 ml/2 tbsp tomato purée (paste)
Salt and freshly ground black pepper
30 ml/2 tbsp sesame seeds, toasted

TO SERVE:
Couscous and a crisp green salad

1   Trim off all excess fat from the chicken and rub all over with the lemon.

2   Heat the butter in a frying pan, add the chicken and brown quickly. Transfer to the crock pot with a draining spoon.

3   Add the onions and pepper to the pan and fry, stirring, for 2 minutes. Tip into the crock pot. Add all the remaining ingredients except the sesame seeds and stir well. Cover and cook on High for 3 hours or Low for 6 hours until everything is tender and bathed in sauce.

4   Taste and re-season if necessary. Sprinkle with the sesame seeds and serve hot with couscous and a green salad.

BEEF DISHES

Cheaper cuts of beef need long, slow cooking not only to make them tender but, particularly when using spices, to impart the rich depth of flavour you want to achieve. A slow cooker does this perfectly, whether you want a powerful Mexican chilli or a more mellow Thai curry. In this section, you'll find every recipe you could possibly want for some wonderful spicy beef dishes.

This is my version of keema, *a curry eaten all over India. It was given to me by a London spice merchant back in the mid-1970s. I've added cream, which makes a richer dish but you can omit it if you prefer. It is also nice with two handfuls of thawed frozen peas added for the last 5–10 minutes. This mild dish is a great way to introduce children to the taste of curry.*

Mild minced beef curry

SERVES 4

30 ml/2 tbsp sunflower oil
2 onions, chopped
2 garlic cloves, crushed
10 ml/2 tsp grated fresh root ginger
450 g/1 lb minced (ground) beef
30 ml/2 tbsp curry powder
200 ml/7 fl oz/scant 1 cup water

30 ml/2 tbsp tomato purée (paste)
Salt
60 ml/4 tbsp double (heavy) cream
  (optional)

TO SERVE:
Plain rice and mango chutney

1 Heat the oil in a saucepan. Add the onions, garlic, ginger and beef and cook, stirring, until the meat is no longer pink and all the grains are separate.

2 Stir in the curry powder and cook for 2 minutes.

3 Stir in the water and tomato purée. Season to taste with salt. Bring to the boil and tip into the crock pot. Cover and cook on High for 2–3 hours.

4 Stir in the cream, if using, taste and re-season if necessary. Serve with rice and mango chutney.

Rezala is quite a dry curry, so I like to add a moister accompanying dish such as a mixed vegetable curry or dhal as well as rice or naan bread. Slow cooking means it isn't as dry as when cooked conventionally, which is all to the good in my opinion! If you prefer, you can discard the bay leaves, cinnamon stick and cardamom pods before serving.

Bangladeshi beef curry

SERVES 4

75 g/3 oz/⅓ cup ghee or butter
2 onions, sliced
1 large garlic clove, crushed
700 g/1½ lb braising steak, cut into cubes
3 bay leaves
7.5 ml/1½ tsp hot chilli powder
1 piece of cinnamon stick
4 cardamom pods

1.5 ml/¼ tsp ground cloves
5 ml/1 tsp caster (superfine) sugar
5 ml/1 tsp salt
350 ml/12 fl oz/1½ cups thick plain yoghurt
Wedges of lemon to garnish

TO SERVE:
Plain rice and side salads

1 Heat the ghee or butter in a saucepan. Add the onions and garlic and fry, stirring, for 2 minutes. Add the beef and continue to fry, turning and stirring, until the beef is browned all over. Tip into the crock pot.

2 Add all the remaining ingredients to the pan and bring to the boil, stirring. Tip into the crock pot. Stir, cover and cook on High for 5 hours or Low for 10 hours until the meat is really tender. For a dryer result, remove the lid and cook on High for a further 30 minutes to thicken the sauce so the ghee floats to the surface.

3 Serve garnished with wedges of lemon with rice and side salads.

This is a simple curry using commercial red curry paste as most are very good. It means you can throw it together in record time then await the delectable results later in the day. All you need to do is cook some rice when it's time to dish up. For even less effort, you can omit browning the ingredients first, but the flavour won't be quite as good.

Thai red beef curry

SERVES 4

30 ml/2 tbsp sunflower oil
2 garlic cloves, crushed
1 onion, roughly chopped
700 g/1½ lb braising beef, cut into
   large cubes
2 large potatoes, peeled and cut into
   fairly large chunks
45 ml/3 tbsp Thai red curry paste
5 ml/1 tsp caster (superfine) sugar
400 g/14 oz/1 large can of coconut
   milk

2 thin red chillies, halved lengthways
   and seeded, if preferred
Salt and freshly ground black pepper
50 g/2 oz/½ cup raw cashew nuts
4 tomatoes, quartered
A few coriander (cilantro) leaves and
   wedges of lime to garnish

TO SERVE:
Thai jasmine rice

1 Heat the oil in a pan. Add the garlic, onion and meat and cook, stirring and turning, for about 3 minutes until the meat is browned. Transfer to the crock pot and add the potatoes.

2 Blend the curry paste with the sugar and coconut milk in the pan. Add the chillies and season to taste. Bring to the boil and pour over the meat. Cover and cook on High for 4–5 hours or Low for 8–10 hours.

3 Add the nuts and tomatoes, pushing them down well into the sauce, cover and cook for 30 minutes more.

4 Serve spooned over jasmine rice in bowls and garnish each bowl with a few coriander leaves and a wedge of lime.

Rendang daging is a rich, creamy Malaysian curry bursting with fragrant spice flavours. It is often made with an expensive cut of meat but stewing beef is rendered meltingly tender by slow cooking. If you have trouble finding thick coconut milk, add about 25 g/1 oz of creamed coconut with the coconut milk.

Rich beef and coconut curry

SERVES 4

1 small onion, roughly chopped
1 large garlic clove, chopped
2.5 cm/1 in piece of fresh root
   ginger, chopped
5 ml/1 tsp crushed dried chillies
15 ml/1 tbsp water
30 ml/2 tbsp groundnut (peanut) or
   vegetable oil
30 ml/2 tbsp desiccated (shredded)
   coconut
400 g/14 oz/1 large can of thick
   coconut milk

1 piece of cinnamon stick
2 whole cloves
2 cardamom pods, split
2 star anise
5 ml/1 tsp palm or caster
   (superfine) sugar
700 g/1½ lb lean stewing beef,
   cubed
Salt

TO SERVE:
Plain rice and green peas

1   Using a pestle and mortar or a bowl and the end of a rolling pin, crush the onion, garlic, ginger and chillies to a paste with the water. Alternatively, use a hand blender.

2   Heat the oil in a frying pan, add the desiccated coconut and fry for 30 seconds until just turning golden. Add the spice paste and fry for 30 seconds, stirring.

3   Add the coconut milk, the remaining spices and the sugar and bring to the boil.

4   Put the beef in the crock pot and add the coconut mixture. Cover and cook on High for 4 hours or Low for 8 hours until tender and just bathed in the coconut (the mixture should be quite dry).

5   Stir well and season to taste with salt. Serve with rice mixed with cooked green peas.

This is a hot, authentic-style beef chilli, similar to a West Indian chilli –
except that it would have red kidney beans instead of pinto beans.
Mexicans laugh when we call this dish chilli con carne, because that,
literally, means chillies with meat – so they envisage a whole bowl of
chillies, just garnished with chopped beef!

Mexican carne con chilli

SERVES 4

15 ml/1 tbsp groundnut (peanut) oil
450 g/1 lb minced (ground) beef
1 large onion, chopped
1 green (bell) pepper, chopped
1 large garlic clove, crushed
400 g/14 oz/1 large can of chopped
  tomatoes
½ x 200 g/7 oz/small jar of pickled
  jalapeno peppers, drained and
  chopped

5–10 ml/1–2 tsp hot chilli powder
1 beef stock cube
2 x 400 g/14 oz/large cans of pinto
  beans (not drained)
Salt and freshly ground black pepper

TO SERVE:
Grated cheese, finely chopped onion
  (mixed with some fresh chopped
  chillies, if liked) and corn tortilla
  chips

1 Heat the oil in a saucepan, add the beef and onion and fry, stirring,
until the onion is browned and the meat is no longer pink and all
the grains are separate.

2 Add all the remaining ingredients and bring to the boil. Tip into
the crock pot, cover and cook on High for 2–3 hours or Low for
4–6 hours.

3 Taste and re-season, if necessary. Serve with grated cheese,
chopped onion and corn tortilla chips.

This is an everyday Tex Mex recipe that should prove popular with all the family. You can use less or more chilli powder according to your own preference. I have suggested cooking on Low, which gives by far the best results, but if time is limited it can be cooked on High for half the time. Try it spooned into crispy tacos or rolled in flour tortillas too.

Traditional chilli con carne

SERVES 4 OR 5

1 onion, chopped
1 garlic clove, chopped
450 g/1 lb minced (ground) beef
2.5 ml/½ tsp hot chilli powder
5 ml/1 tsp ground cumin
5 ml/1 tsp dried oregano
400 g/14 oz/1 large can of chopped tomatoes
2 x 400 g/14 oz/large cans of red kidney beans, drained

15 ml/1 tbsp tomato purée (paste)
90 ml/6 tbsp water
5 ml/1 tsp caster (superfine) sugar
Salt and freshly ground black pepper

TO SERVE:
Plain rice, hot chilli sauce, grated Cheddar cheese and shredded lettuce

1 Put the onion, garlic and mince in a pan and fry, stirring, until the mince grains are separate and no longer pink.

2 Stir in all the remaining ingredients and bring to the boil. Tip in to the crock pot, cover and cook on Low for 6–8 hours.

3 Taste and re-season, if necessary. Serve hot with rice, hot chilli sauce, grated Cheddar and shredded lettuce.

This Cuban speciality is called picadillo *and is often served with fried plantains and rice or a cucumber salad. I first had it in Havana but wasn't sure about the fried plantains! I like it just as it is with lots of flat breads to help mop up the juices and a green salad to cleanse the palate afterwards. You can use the liquid from the drained beef as stock for soup, if you like.*

Spiced chopped beef with olives, raisins and fried eggs

SERVES 4

700 g/1½ lb lean braising steak, cut into large cubes
Salt and freshly ground black pepper
30 ml/2 tbsp sunflower oil, plus extra for frying
1 large onion, finely chopped
1 large garlic clove, finely chopped
2 large green (bell) peppers, finely chopped
1 fat green chilli, seeded, if preferred, and finely chopped

A good pinch of ground cloves
400 g/14 oz/1 large can of chopped tomatoes
5 ml/1 tsp caster (superfine) sugar
50 g/2 oz/⅓ cup stuffed green olives
50 g/2 oz/⅓ cup raisins
10 ml/2 tsp distilled white vinegar
4 eggs
15 ml/1 tbsp chopped fresh coriander (cilantro)

1 Put the beef in the crock pot with a little salt and pepper and cover with boiling water. Cook on High for 4 hours or Low for 8 hours until meltingly tender.

2 About 30 minutes before the beef will be ready, heat the oil in a saucepan. Add the onion and fry, stirring, for 5 minutes.

3 Add all the remaining ingredients except the eggs and coriander. Bring to the boil and boil rapidly for about 5 minutes, stirring occasionally, until thick and pulpy. Season to taste.

4 When the beef is cooked, drain it well and chop it up. Stir it into the tomato mixture and heat through.

5 Heat about 5 mm/¼ in of oil in a frying pan, add the eggs and fry them to your liking.

6 Spoon the beef mixture into shallow bowls, sprinkle with the coriander and top with the eggs.

This is another delightfully fragrant curry, reminiscent of Thai cooking but with the addition of soy sauce, which gives it more earthiness than Thai flavours alone. Don't be tempted to add salt, though you can increase the soy if your taste buds demand it. The long list of ingredients may seem intimidating, but actually the recipe is simplicity itself to prepare.

Malaysian braised beef and potatoes

SERVES 4

10 ml/2 tsp ground coriander
10 ml/2 tsp ground cumin
2.5 ml/½ tsp ground cinnamon
2.5 ml/½ tsp hot chilli powder
1.5 ml/¼ tsp ground cardamom
1.5 ml/¼ tsp ground turmeric
1.5 ml/¼ tsp ground cloves
5 ml/1 tsp crushed dried red chillies
2 stalks of lemon grass, finely chopped
700 g/1½ lb braising steak, cubed
30 ml/2 tbsp groundnut (peanut) oil
2 onions, halved and thinly sliced

2 garlic cloves, crushed
2.5 cm/1 in piece of fresh root ginger, grated
2 large potatoes, peeled and cut into walnut-sized pieces
400 g/14 oz/1 large can of coconut milk
30 ml/2 tbsp soy sauce
5 ml/1 tsp palm or light brown sugar
Salt and freshly ground black pepper

TO SERVE:
Plain rice

1 Mix together the ground spices with the crushed chillies and lemon grass. Add the beef and toss well to coat.

2 Heat the oil in a large pan, add the onions and beef and fry, stirring, for 4 minutes, until richly golden.

3 Add the garlic and ginger and fry for 30 seconds.

4 Put the potatoes in the crock pot and add the beef mixture.

5 Put the coconut milk in the pan and add the soy sauce and sugar. Bring to the boil and pour over the meat. Cover and cook on High for 4 hours or Low for 8 hours until really tender.

6 Season to taste and add more soy sauce, if necessary. Serve with plain boiled rice.

This meat mixture is so versatile. You can serve it in flour tortillas or crispy tacos or as a filling for rolls or pitta breads but I like it best served as below, spooned over avocado on ciabatta slices. My preference is to moisten the meat with enough stock for it to be just coated in sauce, but others like it dryer. Add more jalapeno peppers if you dare!

Mexican shredded meats with chorizo

SERVES 4

450 g/1 lb lean braising steak, cut into 5 cm/2 in chunks
4 lean belly pork slices
1 onion, quartered
2 bay leaves
1 sprig of fresh rosemary
600 ml/1 pt/2½ cups boiling water
5 ml/1 tsp salt
Freshly ground black pepper
100 g/4 oz piece of chorizo sausage, skinned and sliced
100 g/4 oz tomatillos, fresh or drained canned (or green or unripe tomatoes), roughly chopped

2 sun-dried tomatoes, roughly chopped
30 ml/2 tbsp tomato purée (paste)
50 g/2 oz pickled sliced jalapeno peppers
5 ml/1 tsp dried oregano

TO SERVE:
1 ciabatta loaf, split in 4 lengthways
2 ripe avocados, halved, stoned (pitted) and peeled
Juice of 1 lime
50 g/2 oz/½ cup crumbled Queso Fresco or Feta cheese (optional)
Shredded lettuce

1 Put the steak and pork in the crock pot with the onion, bay leaves and rosemary. Add the boiling water, salt and lots of pepper. Cover and cook on High for 4 hours or Low for 8 hours until the meat is meltingly tender.

2 Lift the meats out of the pot (reserve the stock). Discard any excess fat, skin or bones, then shred the meat between two forks.

3 Heat a non-stick frying pan and fry the chorizo until the fat runs. Add the shredded meats and all the remaining ingredients, adding enough of the reserved stock to moisten the mixture to your liking. Cook, stirring, for 5 minutes until the tomatillos are softened and everything is moist and flavoursome. Taste and re-season, if necessary.

4 Meanwhile, toast the ciabatta slices. Mash the avocados with the lime juice.

5 Put the bread on four plates and spread the mashed avocado over. Spoon the meat mixture over and scatter with the cheese, if using. Serve straight away with shredded lettuce.

Ropa vieja is usually served with the ubiquitous rice and peas, which is really plain boiled rice mixed with black eyed beans or red kidney beans. It's also good served with couscous. My recipe here is much less fiery than other versions, but this means you get the full flavour of the capers. I like it best with a large cucumber salad to round off the meal.

Cuban spicy beef

SERVES 4

30 ml/2 tbsp corn or vegetable oil
2 large onions, finely chopped
1 large carrot, finely chopped
1 green (bell) pepper, finely chopped
1 large garlic clove, finely chopped
2 fat red chillies, seeded, if
   preferred, and chopped
5 ml/1 tsp ground turmeric
A good pinch of ground cloves
A good pinch of ground cinnamon

15 ml/1 tbsp pickled capers, chopped
400 g/14 oz/1 large can of chopped
   tomatoes
150 ml/¼ pt/⅔ cup beef stock
Salt and freshly ground black pepper
700 g/1½ lb piece of braising steak,
   trimmed and cut into 4 equal
   pieces
1 large pimiento, from a can or jar,
   drained and chopped

1 Heat the oil in a pan, add the onions and carrot and fry, stirring, for 2 minutes. Add all the remaining ingredients except the steak and pimiento and bring to the boil.

2 Lay the steak in the crock pot in a single layer (if possible) and pour the boiling mixture over. Cover and cook on High for 5 hours or Low for 10 hours until meltingly tender and bathed in a rich sauce.

3 Taste and re-season if necessary. Serve generously sprinkled with the chopped pimiento.

The authentic stew doesn't have chillies but I find that adding them at the end of cooking adds an exciting extra dimension to the dish. The star anise brings a warm earthiness too. It is amazing how the addition of tamari (Japanese soy sauce) can add so much flavour! If you can't get daikon, use two turnips instead.

Japanese beef stew with shredded chillies

SERVES 4

700 g/1½ lb braising steak, cut into finger-width strips
1 bunch of spring onions (scallions), cut into short diagonal lengths
2 large carrots, diced
½ daikon, diced
2 potatoes, diced
100 g/4 oz shiitake mushrooms, thickly sliced
25 g/1 oz/2 tbsp palm or light brown sugar
30 ml/2 tbsp tamari

10 ml/2 tsp pickled ginger, finely chopped
150 ml/¼ pt/⅔ cup beef stock
75 ml/5 tbsp sake or dry white wine
1 star anise
100 g/4 oz mangetout (snow peas)
2 fat red chillies, seeded and thinly shredded
2 fat green chillies, seeded and thinly shredded

TO SERVE:
Rice noodles

1 Put the beef and vegetables in the crock pot. Mix the sugar with the tamari, ginger, stock and sake or wine in a saucepan. Bring to the boil and pour over the beef and vegetables. Add the star anise.

2 Cover and cook on High for 4 hours or Low for 8 hours. Add the mangetout and cook for a further 1 hour.

3 Stir in the shredded chillies. Taste and add a dash more tamari, if liked. Discard the star anise and serve spooned over rice noodles.

This Mexican recipe is similar to a beef chilli but is enriched with cocoa powder. It packs quite a punch but is gently toned down by serving it on a bed of vermicelli and smothering it in Montery Jack cheese. If you really feel the heat will be more than you will be comfortable with, halve the chilli powder and omit the fresh chillies altogether.

Chilli beef mole with fine noodles

SERVES 4

1 onion, finely chopped
500 g/18 oz lean minced (ground)
   beef
2.5 ml/½ tsp ground allspice
1.5 ml/¼ tsp ground cloves
5 ml/1 tsp ground cinnamon
5 ml/1 tsp ground cumin
2.5 ml/½ tsp hot chilli powder
2 fat green chillies, seeded, if
   preferred, and chopped
100 g/4 oz tomato purée (paste)
10 ml/2 tsp cocoa (unsweetened
   chocolate) powder

150 ml/¼ pt/⅔ cup water
¼ x 170 g/6 oz jar of pickled
   jalapeno peppers, drained
10 ml/2 tsp Worcestershire sauce
400 g/14 oz/1 large can of red
   kidney beans
Salt

TO SERVE:
Vermicelli, thinly sliced red onions,
   grated Montery Jack cheese

1 Dry-fry the onion and beef in a saucepan, stirring, until the beef is no longer pink and all the grains are separate.

2 Add all the spices and cook for 30 seconds. Stir in all the remaining ingredients, including the kidney bean liquor, and season to taste with salt. Bring to the boil, then tip into the crock pot. Cover and cook on High for 2–3 hours or Low for 4–6 hours until rich and tender.

3 Taste and re-season, if necessary. Serve on a bed of cooked vermicelli, with thinly sliced red onions and lots of grated Montery Jack cheese.

LAMB
DISHES

Lamb takes on a sweet succulence when slow cooked and, if blended with various spices from fiery chillies to warm cinnamon and cumin, you'll find it is difficult to beat. I sometimes just call for lean diced lamb. I prefer to buy fresh shoulder and cut it up myself but if you buy it frozen, ready-prepared, I recommend you not only thaw it out before use but also pick it over carefully, as it can be fatty and sometimes also rather sinewy, so it may be false economy.

Palak gosht is a Northern Indian dish that uses lamb neck fillets, which are so tender it doesn't take as long to cook as some curries. You can use diced chicken breast instead of the lamb if you prefer. Make sure you cut up the carrots quite small so they become really tender. The rice, chutney and pickle accompaniments are all this curry needs to make a delicious dish.

Lamb, spinach and raisin curry

SERVES 4

15 ml/1 tbsp groundnut (peanut) or sunflower oil
1 large onion, chopped
1 carrot, finely chopped
1 garlic clove, crushed
700 g/1½ lb lamb neck fillet, cut into chunky slices
5 ml/1 tsp grated fresh root ginger
30 ml/2 tbsp mild curry paste

5 ml/1 tsp paprika
1 small piece of cinnamon stick
5 ml/1 tsp salt
450 g/1 lb fresh spinach
25 g/1 oz/3 tbsp raisins

TO SERVE:
Pilau rice, mango chutney and lime pickle

1 Heat the oil in a saucepan. Add the onion, carrot and garlic and fry, stirring, for 2 minutes. Add the lamb, ginger, curry paste, paprika, cinnamon and salt and cook, stirring, until the meat is browned on all sides. Tip into the crock pot.

2 Wash the spinach thoroughly and shake off the excess moisture. Roughly chop and add to the crock pot with the raisins. Cover and cook on High for 2–3 hours or Low for 4–6 hours.

3 Discard the cinnamon stick, taste and re-season if necessary. Serve with pilau rice, mango chutney and lime pickle.

There are many different versions of biryani *– a meat and rice dish – but they're not normally cooked in a slow cooker and some recipes can be complicated and time consuming. This is my adaptation of a conventionally cooked recipe and it works extremely well. The rice is cooked separately to keep the grains fluffy. Try it with chicken instead of lamb, too.*

Lamb and coconut biryani

SERVES 4

25 g/1 oz/2 tbsp ghee or butter
2 large onions, thinly sliced
500 g/18 oz lean diced lamb
5 ml/1 tsp ground ginger
1.5–2.5 ml/¼–½ tsp hot chilli powder
2 cardamom pods
2 pieces of cinnamon stick
1 bay leaf, torn in half
2.5 ml/½ tsp salt
5 ml/1 tsp grated fresh root ginger
2.5 ml/½ tsp coarsely ground black pepper
1.5 ml/¼ tsp caraway seeds

5 ml/1 tsp garam masala
120 ml/4 fl oz/½ cup plain yoghurt
350 g/12 oz/1½ cups basmati rice
50 g/2 oz/½ cup frozen peas (optional)
60 ml/4 tbsp currants and 60 ml/ 4 tbsp desiccated (shredded) coconut to garnish

TO SERVE:
Popadoms, a side salad, raita (see page 107), lime pickle and mango chutney

1   Heat the ghee or butter in a saucepan. Add the onions and fry, stirring, for 3–4 minutes until golden. Transfer to the crock pot with a draining spoon.

2   Add the lamb to the pan and brown on all sides. Add all the spices, the bay leaf, salt, ginger, pepper, caraway seeds and garam masala and cook, stirring, for 1 minute. Stir in the yoghurt and tip into the crock pot. Cover and cook on High for 4 hours or Low for 8 hours.

3   Meanwhile, cook the rice according to the packet directions, adding the peas, if using, for the last 5 minutes' cooking. Drain.

4   When the meat is cooked, add the cooked rice and fork through. Serve garnished with the currants and desiccated coconut with popadoms, salad, raita, lime pickle and mango chutney.

Korma is a mild but rich, creamy curry, which is also lovely when made with chicken. Stirring in the garam masala at the end really lifts the whole thing and the coriander adds a lovely fragrance. It's a tasty but gentle curry suitable for serving to younger members of the family but if they don't like coriander, as with some of my own family, you can use torn fresh basil leaves.

Creamy lamb and almond curry

SERVES 4

2 large garlic cloves, crushed
5 ml/1 tsp grated fresh root ginger
50 g/2 oz/½ cup ground almonds
200 ml/7 fl oz/scant 1 cup water
30 ml/2 tbsp groundnut (peanut) oil
700 g/1½ lbs lean diced lamb
1 large onion, finely chopped
4 cardamom pods, split
5 ml/1 tsp ground cumin
5 ml/1 tsp ground coriander
2.5 ml/½ tsp ground cinnamon
1.5 ml/¼ tsp hot chilli powder

A good pinch of ground cloves
10 ml/2 tsp caster (superfine) sugar
Salt and freshly ground black pepper
60 ml/4 tbsp crème fraîche or single
  (light) cream
2.5 ml/½ tsp garam masala
Wedges of lemon and torn coriander
  (cilantro) leaves to garnish

TO SERVE:
Pilau rice and a green salad

1   Mash the garlic with the ginger and almonds, then mix with 60 ml/4 tbsp of the water to form a paste.

2   Heat the oil in a large frying pan, add the meat in batches and fry until browned all over. Transfer the meat to the crock pot with a draining spoon.

3   Add the onion to the pan and fry, stirring, for 2–3 minutes until turning golden. Scrape the cardamom seeds into the pan and stir in the cumin, coriander, cinnamon, chilli, cloves, sugar and the almond paste and cook, stirring, for 30 seconds.

4 Blend in the remaining water and bring to the boil, stirring. Season to taste with salt and pepper. Pour into the crock pot, stir, cover and cook on High for 3 hours or Low for 6 hours until the lamb is really tender.

5 Stir in the crème fraîche or cream and garam masala, taste and re-season, if necessary. Garnish with wedges of lemon and torn coriander leaves and serve with pilau rice and a green salad.

Rogan josh takes its rich red colour from the paprika and chilli powder, with a splash of tomato purée for good measure. As ever, there are hundreds of different versions of this succulent dish. Mine has fennel seeds and asafoetida for added fragrance but it's still a good curry even without them so you can omit them if you prefer.

Kashmir red lamb stew

SERVES 4

15 ml/1 tbsp fennel seeds	5 ml/1 tsp palm or light brown sugar
30 ml/2 tbsp groundnut (peanut) oil	15 ml/1 tbsp tomato purée (paste)
700 g/1½ lb lean diced lamb	90 ml/6 tbsp plain yoghurt
2.5 ml/½ tsp ground cinnamon	150 ml/¼ pt/⅔ cup water
5 ml/1 tsp ground ginger	Salt and freshly ground black pepper
30 ml/2 tbsp paprika	45 ml/3 tbsp roughly chopped fresh
2.5 ml/½ tsp hot chilli powder	coriander (cilantro) leaves
1.5 ml/¼ tsp ground cloves	
2.5 ml/½ tsp garam masala	TO SERVE:
A good pinch of asafoetida	Basmati rice, lime pickle and mango
1 bay leaf	chutney

1 Roughly crush the fennel seeds using a pestle and mortar, or in a bowl with the end of a rolling pin, to release their aroma. Heat the oil in a saucepan, add the lamb and fry on all sides to brown.

2 Add the fennel and all the other spices, the bay leaf and sugar and fry, stirring, for 1 minute. Tip into the crock pot.

3 Add the tomato purée, yoghurt and water to the pan and bring to the boil, stirring (it will curdle). Pour over the lamb, season with a little salt and pepper and stir well. Cover and cook on High for 3 hours or Low for 6 hours until meltingly tender and bathed in a rich sauce.

4 Taste and re-season if necessary. Stir in the coriander and serve spooned over basmati rice, with lime pickle and mango chutney.

You can cheat with this popular dish and use 45–60 ml/3–4 tbsp of Madras curry paste instead of making your own, then continue from step 2. Blending your own is very satisfying, though, and the flavour is superior to any ready-made product! Try this recipe with chicken or beef too, but for beef cook for 4–5 hours on High or 8–10 hours on Low.

Madras lamb curry

SERVES 4

2 cardamom pods, split
5 ml/1 tsp coriander seeds
5 ml/1 tsp cumin seeds
5 ml/1 tsp black peppercorns
5 ml/1 tsp crushed dried chillies
10 ml/2 tsp grated fresh root ginger
2 onions

2 large garlic cloves, chopped
30 ml/2 tbsp tomato purée (paste)
2.5 ml/½ tsp salt
700 g/1½ lb lean diced lamb
25 g/1 oz/2 tbsp ghee or butter
300 ml/½ pt/1¼ cups plain yoghurt

1   Scrape the seeds from the cardamom pods. Crush the seeds and all the other spices using a pestle and mortar, or in a small bowl with the end of a rolling pin. Chop one of the onions and add to the bowl with the garlic. Pound again to form a rough paste (or use a hand blender). Add the tomato purée and salt.

2   Put the lamb in a sealable container. Add the spice paste, mix with the hands to coat the meat, then cover and leave to marinate for at least 2 hours, or even overnight.

3   Slice the remaining onion. Heat the ghee or butter in a pan, add the onion and fry for 3 minutes until lightly browned. Remove with a draining spoon and put in the crock pot.

4   Add the lamb to the pan and brown on all sides. Stir in the yoghurt, bring to the boil and tip into the crock pot. Stir, cover and cook on High for 3 hours or Low for 6 hours until really tender and bathed in a rich sauce.

5   Taste and re-season, if necessary, before serving.

I love Greek-style lamb dishes, flavoured with garlic and herbs and slow roasted on the bone for hours until meltingly tender. I've created a spicy version, influenced by Indian cuisine, for this book and it works a dream. The meat is served in large, tender chunks, bathed in a rich, thick sauce. Serve with naans, chapattis or any other Indian breads of your choice.

Indian-style slow-roast leg of lamb

SERVES 4

1 garlic clove, peeled and crushed
1 cm/½ in piece of fresh root ginger, grated
25 g/1 oz/¼ cup ground almonds
2 fat green chillies, seeded, if preferred, and finely chopped
15 ml/1 tbsp paprika
A good pinch of ground cloves
5 ml/1 tsp salt
5 ml/1 tsp palm or light brown sugar
200 ml/7 fl oz/scant 1 cup plain yoghurt

½ leg of lamb, about 900g/2 lb
30 ml/2 tbsp groundnut (peanut) oil
1 onion, thinly sliced
5 ml/1 tsp cumin seeds
5 ml/1 tsp black mustard seeds
2 cardamom pods, split
1 piece of cinnamon stick
Freshly ground black pepper
30 ml/2 tbsp boiling water

TO SERVE:
Indian breads, a selection of chutneys and a mixed salad

1   Mix the garlic with the ginger, almonds, chillies, paprika, cloves, salt, sugar and yoghurt.

2   Make deep cuts in the lamb using a sharp knife. Put the lamb in the crock pot and smear the yoghurt mixture all over, pushing it well into the slits with your fingers.

3   Heat the oil in a frying pan, add the onion and fry for 4 minutes, stirring, until golden. Add the cumin and mustard seeds, cardamom pods, cinnamon stick and pepper and cook until the seeds begin to 'pop'. Spoon this mixture over the lamb. Add the water to the crock pot.

4 Cover and cook on High for 5 hours or Low for 10 hours, by which time the lamb should be meltingly tender and a rich sauce will have formed.

5 Lift the meat out of the pot. Spoon off excess fat from the sauce, if necessary. Stir the sauce well, thin with a little water, taste and re-season if necessary. Serve the lamb cut into chunky pieces with the sauce spooned over, Indian breads, a selection of chutneys and a mixed salad.

This is my mild version of a dopiaza curry – it's served much hotter in many restaurants. Traditionally, the whole spices are left in the serving dish to be fished out by the recipient. The green beans are not exactly authentic, but they do taste so good! These quantities make generous servings for four people; for six you could include a couple of side dishes.

Lamb and bean curry with whole spices

SERVES 4–6

5 ml/1 tsp coriander seeds
5 ml/1 tsp cumin seeds
5 ml/1 tsp black mustard seeds
5 ml/1 tsp black peppercorns
1.5 ml/¼ tsp crushed dried chillies
1 small onion, quartered
3 garlic cloves, peeled
2.5 cm/1 in piece of fresh root
 ginger, chopped
150 ml/¼ pt/⅔ cup water
60 ml/4 tbsp groundnut (peanut) oil
700 g/1½ lb lean diced lamb
120 ml/4 fl oz/½ cup plain yoghurt
1 piece of cinnamon stick

4 whole cloves
6 cardamom pods, split
Salt
100 g/4 oz thin French (green)
 beans, topped, tailed and cut into
 thirds
3 large onions, halved and thinly
 sliced
5 ml/1 tsp garam masala

TO SERVE:
Plain naan breads and mango
 chutney

1 Grind the coriander, cumin and mustard seeds with the peppercorns and chilli flakes using a pestle and mortar, or in a bowl with the end of a rolling pin. Alternatively, use a hand blender. Add the onion quarters, the garlic and ginger and pound until a fairly smooth paste has formed. Blend in 90 ml/6 tbsp of the water.

2 Heat half the oil in a frying pan, add the lamb and fry on all sides to brown. Transfer to the crock pot with a draining spoon.

3 Add the spice paste to the frying pan and fry, stirring, for 1 minute. Add the remaining water and the yoghurt. Bring to the boil, stirring, then pour over the lamb. Add the whole spices and a little salt and stir well.

4 Cover and cook on High for 3 hours or Low for 6 hours until meltingly tender and bathed in a rich sauce.

5 Meanwhile, boil the beans in a little water or steam for 5 minutes until just tender. Drain. Fry the sliced onions in the remaining oil for 4–5 minutes until brown and soft. Drain on kitchen paper (paper towels).

6 When the curry is cooked, spoon off the excess oil, stir in the beans, fried onions and garam masala, taste and add more salt, if necessary. Leave to stand for 5 minutes, then serve with plain naan breads and mango chutney.

Koftas are often a bit dry, but cooking them in the slow cooker in a yoghurt stock makes them really moist and succulent. Use a Greek-style yoghurt, not a set one, or you'll have curds remaining when the dish is cooked. Try it with lean minced beef instead of lamb, and use papaya instead of mango in the sambal – or even pork with fresh pineapple.

Kofta meatballs with fresh mango, mint and cucumber sambal

SERVES 4

700 g/1½ lbs lean minced (ground) lamb
1 large garlic clove, crushed
5 ml/1 tsp ground cumin
5 ml/1 tsp ground coriander
1.5 ml/¼ tsp hot chilli powder
1.5 ml/¼ tsp ground cloves
1.5 ml/¼ tsp ground nutmeg
Salt and freshly ground black pepper
1 egg, beaten
2 bay leaves
1 piece of cinnamon stick
2 whole cloves
2 cardamom pods, split
90 ml/6 tbsp boiling water

90 ml/6 tbsp plain yoghurt

FOR THE SAMBAL:
1 small mango
1 small red onion, finely chopped
5 cm/2 in piece of cucumber, finely chopped
30 ml/2 tbsp chopped fresh mint
15 ml/1 tbsp chopped fresh coriander (cilantro)
Juice of 1 lime
5 ml/1 tsp crushed dried chillies

TO SERVE:
Basmati rice

1   Mix the lamb and garlic with the ground spices and a little salt and pepper. Work in the beaten egg to bind. With wet hands, shape the mixture into sausage shapes about 7.5 cm/3 in long. Place in the crock pot and tuck the bay leaves, cinnamon stick, cloves and cardamom pods around.

2   Mix together the boiling water and yoghurt until smooth, then spoon over the lamb. Cover and cook on High for 2 hours or Low for 4 hours until the meatballs are cooked through (the liquid will look slightly unappetising but, don't worry, you don't eat it!).

3 Meanwhile, to make the sambal, cut the flesh and skin off the mango stone (pit) in thick slices, following the contour of the stone. Score the flesh through to the skin one way, then the other, to make small dice. Bend back the skin and cut off the flesh. Place in a bowl and mix with the remaining ingredients. Chill until ready to serve.

4 When the koftas are cooked, gently lift them out of the liquid with a draining spoon and transfer to warm plates. Serve with basmati rice and the sambal.

*This internationally acclaimed South African curry with a custard topping
is usually baked, but I've found it cooks perfectly in the slow cooker.
A friend introduced me to the sweet potato topping and I've used it ever
since as it it adds a lovely extra dimension. However, if you prefer, omit it
and just sprinkle the custard with the toasted coconut.*

Bobotie

SERVES 4

1 thick slice of wholemeal bread
250 ml/8 fl oz/1 cup milk
30 ml/2 tbsp groundnut (peanut) oil
2 onions, chopped
450 g/1 lb minced (ground) lamb
30 ml/2 tbsp mild curry powder
15 ml/1 tbsp lemon juice
15 ml/1 tbsp apricot jam (conserve)
8 ready-to-eat dried apricots,
   chopped
50 g/2 oz/⅓ cup raisins
50 g/2 oz/½ cup flaked (slivered)
   almonds
2.5 ml/½ tsp dried basil

Salt and freshly ground black pepper
2 eggs, beaten
150 ml/¼ pt/⅔ cup single (light)
   cream
A pinch of ground nutmeg
2 sweet potatoes, cut into small
   chunks
A small knob of butter
15 ml/1 tbsp desiccated (shredded)
   coconut

TO SERVE:
Plain rice, mango or another sweet
   chutney and a crisp green salad

1 Soak the bread in the milk.

2 Heat the oil in a saucepan, add the onions and lamb and fry,
stirring, until the meat is no longer pink and all the grains are
separate. Stir in the curry powder and cook for 1 minute, stirring.
Remove from the heat.

3 Beat the soaked bread and the milk into the meat with the lemon
juice, jam, apricots, raisins, almonds, basil and some salt and
pepper. Place in a deep 20 cm/8 in diameter round dish or put the
mixture directly in a small, round crock pot. Press down well.

4 Beat the eggs with the cream, nutmeg and a little salt and pepper.
Pour over the top. If using a dish, place in the crock pot with
enough boiling water to come half-way up the sides. Cover and
cook on Low for 5–6 hours until set.

5 Meanwhile, boil the sweet potatoes in lightly salted water for about 10 minutes or until tender. Drain and return to the pan. Heat gently to remove any excess moisture, then mash well with the butter and season with pepper.

6 Spoon the mashed sweet potato on top of the bobotie and spread it out evenly. Sprinkle with the coconut and serve with rice, a sweet chutney and a crisp green salad.

Use boned meat if you prefer, though traditionally the bone is left in to add flavour. Get your butcher to chop it for you. Alternatively you could use lamb shanks – expensive but very good! If you can get goat, do try it; the flavour is sensational and it is very low in saturated fat. This dish is traditionally served with rice and peas (black eyed beans) and fried plantain.

Jamaican curried goat or lamb

SERVES 4–6

2 fat red chillies
25 g/1 oz/2 tbsp butter
30 ml/2 tbsp groundnut (peanut) oil
1 kg/2¼ lb shoulder or leg of goat or lamb, on the bone, chopped into large chunks
1 large onion, chopped
30 ml/2 tbsp mild curry powder
1.5 ml/¼ tsp ground allspice
1 large garlic clove, finely chopped

1 tomato, seeded and chopped
400 g/14 oz/1 large can of coconut milk
30 ml/2 tbsp chopped fresh thyme
Salt to taste
Juice of ½ lime
Wedges of lime, to garnish

TO SERVE:
Saffron or plain rice and black eyed beans

1 Seed and chop one of the chillies and leave the other one whole. Heat the butter and oil in a pan, add the meat and brown on all sides. Transfer to the crock pot with a draining spoon.

2 Add the onion to the pan and fry, stirring, for 2 minutes. Stir in the curry powder and allspice and fry for a further minute.

3 Stir in the chopped and whole chilli and all the remaining ingredients, bring to the boil and pour over the meat. Stir, cover and cook on High for 4 hours or Low for 8 hours until meltingly tender. Taste and re-season if necessary.

4 Garnish with wedges of lime and serve with saffron or plain rice and black eyed beans.

The crock pot makes a good alternative to a traditional North African tagine to cook these spicy fruit and meat stews as it keeps moisture in and gently cooks the food until it is richly bathed in sauce. If you can find dried Angelino plums, try them halved instead of the prunes – not authentic, since most come from California, but they make a great tagine!

Minted lamb tagine with prunes

SERVES 4

700 g/1½ lb diced stewing lamb
12 button (pearl) onions, peeled but left whole
2 courgettes (zucchini), diced
2 carrots, diced
1 green (bell) pepper, diced
100 g/4 oz/⅔ cup ready-to-eat stoned (pitted) prunes, halved
1 fat green chilli, seeded, if preferred, and chopped
1 large garlic clove, crushed

1.5 ml/¼ tsp ground cinnamon
1.5 ml/¼ tsp ground ginger
Salt and freshly ground black pepper
450 ml/¾ pts/2 cups boiling lamb or chicken stock
225 g/8 oz/1⅓ cups couscous
30 ml/2 tbsp tomato purée (paste)
30 ml/2 tbsp chopped fresh mint
30 ml/2 tbsp chopped fresh parsley

1 Put the lamb and the prepared vegetables in the crock pot with the prunes, fresh chilli, garlic, the spices and a little salt and pepper. Add the boiling stock, cover and cook on High for 3 hours or Low for 6 hours.

2 Just before the end of the cooking time, put the couscous in a bowl and just cover with boiling water. Place the bowl over a pan of boiling water and leave to steam for 15 minutes.

3 Stir the tomato purée and half the herbs into the tagine. Taste and re-season, if necessary.

4 Spoon the couscous on to serving plates. Spoon the lamb mixture on top and sprinkle with the remaining herbs before serving.

This dish has a wonderful fragrance and is one of our family favourites. You could use a large turnip or a couple of handfuls of whole radishes instead of the daikon, and frozen peas or sliced courgettes could be substituted for the beans. It's equally good made with beef but it would need a longer cooking time – 4–5 hours on High or 8–10 hours on Low.

Saigon spiced lamb stew

SERVES 4

30 ml/2 tbsp groundnut (peanut) oil
2 onions, halved and thinly sliced
2 garlic cloves, crushed
2 large potatoes, cut into chunks
2 large carrots, cut into chunks
½ daikon, cut into chunks
700 g /1½ lb lean diced lamb
10 ml/2 tsp grated fresh root ginger
5 ml/1 tsp mild curry paste
1 piece of cinnamon stick

2 thin red chillies, seeded, if
    preferred, and finely chopped
2 star anise
5 ml/1 tsp palm or light brown sugar
30 ml/2 tbsp tomato purée (paste)
15 ml/1 tbsp Thai fish sauce
300 ml/½ pt /1¼ cups water
Salt and freshly ground black pepper
100 g/4 oz French (green) beans,
    cut into short lengths

1 Heat the oil in a large pan, add the onions and garlic and fry gently for 2 minutes. Transfer to the crock pot with a draining spoon. Add the prepared vegetables to the crock pot.

2 Add the lamb to the pan and fry, stirring, until browned all over. Add all the spices and the sugar and fry for 30 seconds.

3 Add the tomato purée, the fish sauce and water and bring to the boil. Add some salt and pepper and tip it all into the crock pot.

4 Cover and cook on High for 3–4 hours or Low for 6–8 hours until very tender.

5 Just before the end of the cooking time, cook the beans in a little water or steam them for about 5 minutes until just tender but still bright green. When the stew is cooked, remove the whole spices, stir in the beans and serve straight away.

In Chinese cuisine, 'red cooked' simply means cooked in soy sauce as the finished dish has a lovely deep, rich mahogany colour. If you don't have potato flour, cornflour is a good substitute. Blend the same amount of cornflour with the sherry and stir it in for the last 10 minutes' cooking time to thicken the sauce. You can use more chillies if you want more heat.

Chinese chilli red cooked lamb

SERVES 4

700 g/1½ lb lean diced lamb
2 large garlic cloves, crushed
1 bunch of spring onions (scallions), chopped
2 red (bell) peppers, cut into diamond shapes
1 fat red chilli, seeded, if preferred, and chopped
2.5 cm/1 in piece of fresh root ginger, grated
5 ml/1 tsp Chinese five spice powder

15 ml/1 tbsp tomato purée (paste)
15 ml/1 tbsp potato flour
30 ml/2 tbsp dry sherry
75 ml/5 tbsp soy sauce
150 ml/¼ pt/⅔ cup boiling lamb stock
40 g/1½ oz/3 tbsp palm or light brown sugar

TO SERVE:
Plain rice

1 Put the lamb, garlic, spring onions and half the pepper diamonds in the crock pot.

2 Mix together all the remaining ingredients except the remaining pepper and pour over. Stir well, cover and cook on High for 3–4 hours or Low for 6–8 hours until the lamb is tender and bathed in a rich sauce.

3 Serve spooned over boiled rice, garnished with the remaining pepper diamonds.

PORK
DISHES

Pork isn't as obvious a choice as other meats for the spice treatment but all these dishes are exceptionally delicious. Using spices helps to offset the richness of pork and, because if has a robust flavour anyway, it can support deep flavour combinations that make for sensational eating! Here you'll find everything from my Pork Vindaloo – one of the hottest curries I can stand – to some sweet, spicy ribs and a wonderful Cajun-spiced Pork Loin joint.

This delicately flavoured curry is almost a fusion of Chinese and Thai cooking. It's a wonderful dish to choose when you are short of time as there is very little preparation – not even any pounding or frying! Galangal adds an authentic, spicy, ginger-like flavour but you can substitute grated root ginger instead. Add more chillies if you like a hotter curry.

Pork chiang mai curry

SERVES 4

60 ml/4 tbsp yellow bean sauce
45 ml/3 tbsp Thai green curry paste
1 thin green chilli, seeded, if preferred, and chopped
1 onion, grated
1 large garlic clove, crushed
10 ml/2 tsp grated galangal
1 stalk of lemon grass, finely chopped
10 ml/2 tsp tamarind paste
10 ml/2 tsp Thai fish sauce

15 ml/1 tbsp palm or light brown sugar
700 g/1½ lb pork shoulder, cut into strips
400 ml/14 oz/1 large can of coconut milk
Salt and freshly ground black pepper
30 ml/2 tbsp chopped fresh coriander (cilantro)

TO SERVE:
Rice noodles

1 Mix the bean sauce with the curry paste, chilli, onion, garlic, galangal, lemon grass, tamarind paste, fish sauce and sugar in the crock pot. Add the pork and toss well to coat.

2 Bring the coconut milk to the boil in a saucepan and pour over the meat. Stir, cover and cook on High for 3 hours or Low for 6 hours until really tender.

3 Season to taste, sprinkle with the coriander and serve spooned over rice noodles.

This rich curry is thicker than most from the Myanmar region, and the cashew nuts add a lovely texture. I have suggested serving it with turmeric-flavoured jasmine rice to add extra colour. Simply add about 5 ml/1 tsp of ground turmeric to the cooking water and boil as usual. You can add a couple of split cardamom pods to the water, too, if you like.

Myanmar pork curry

SERVES 4

30 ml/2 tbsp groundnut (peanut) or sunflower oil
700 g/1½ lb pork shoulder, cut into thick strips
1 large onion, chopped
1 large garlic clove, crushed
2.5 cm/1 in piece of fresh root ginger, grated
5 ml/1 tsp ground turmeric
5 ml/1 tsp ground cumin

5 ml/1 tsp ground coriander
2.5 ml/½ tsp hot chilli powder
30 ml/2 tbsp soy sauce
5 ml/1 tsp palm or light brown sugar
100 g/4 oz creamed coconut
250 ml/8 fl oz/1 cup boiling water
50 g/2 oz/½ cup raw cashew nuts

TO SERVE:
Turmeric-flavoured jasmine rice

1 Heat the oil in a large frying pan, add the pork and fry until browned. Transfer to the crock pot with a draining spoon.

2 Add the onion to the pan and fry for 2 minutes, stirring, then stir in the garlic, ginger, turmeric, cumin, coriander and chilli powder and fry for 30 seconds, stirring.

3 Blend in the soy sauce, sugar, coconut and water and bring to the boil, stirring, until the coconut melts. Pour over the pork and scatter the nuts over the top. Cover and cook on High for 3 hours or Low for 6 hours until really tender.

4 Serve spooned over turmeric–flavoured jasmine rice.

This recipe comes from Goa, the only region of India where pork is eaten
as it is largely a Christian community. This is a fiery curry and for
authenticity the chillies should not be seeded! You can also make it with
chicken or turkey; simply substitute diced chicken breasts or turkey steaks.
Try stewing beef, too, but cook for 4–5 hours on High or 8–10 hours on Low.

Pork vindaloo

SERVES 4

2 onions, quartered
2 garlic cloves, peeled
2.5 cm/1 in piece of fresh root
    ginger, chopped
3 thin red chillies, seeded, if
    preferred
60 ml/4 tbsp groundnut (peanut) or
    sunflower oil
60 ml/4 tbsp water
2 cardamom pods
5 ml/1 tsp hot chilli powder
1.5 ml/¼ tsp ground cloves
5 ml/1 tsp ground nutmeg
10 ml/2 tsp ground cumin
5 ml/1 tsp palm or light brown sugar

60 ml/4 tbsp malt vinegar
30 ml/2 tbsp tomato purée (paste)
700 g/1½ lb lean pork shoulder, cut
    into large chunks
2 large potatoes, cut into walnut-
    sized pieces
250 ml/8 fl oz/1 cup boiling pork or
    beef stock
Salt and freshly ground black pepper
30 ml/2 tbsp chopped fresh
    coriander (cilantro)

TO SERVE:
Naan breads, plain yoghurt, lime
    pickle and mango chutney

1   Using a small food processor or hand blender, run the machine and
    drop in the onions, garlic, ginger and chillies. Add 30 ml/2 tbsp of
    the oil and all the water and blend until a coarse paste has formed,
    stopping and scraping down the sides as necessary.

2   Split the cardamom pods and add the seeds to the blender with
    the remaining spices, the sugar, vinegar and tomato purée.
    Blend again.

3   Heat the remaining oil in a pan, add the pork and fry until lightly
    browned all over. Add the spice paste and cook over a low heat,
    stirring, for 1 minute.

4 Put the potatoes in the crock pot, then tip in the pork mixture. Stir the boiling stock into the pan, then pour over the pork mixture. Season well. Cover and cook on High for 3–4 hours or Low for 6–8 hours until meltingly tender.

5 Taste and re-season if necessary, then serve sprinkled with the chopped coriander with naan breads, plain yoghurt, lime pickle and mango chutney.

Traditionally, the spinach is added in time for it to cook down completely (as I've done here) but, if you prefer, add the tomatoes for the last hour and the spinach right at the end of the cooking time; stir it in, cover and leave to stand for 5 minutes until it is just wilted. That way you'll retain the bright green colour too.

Thai green pork and spinach curry

SERVES 4

400 g/14 oz/1 large can of coconut milk
30 ml/2 tbsp Thai green curry paste
30 ml/2 tbsp Thai fish sauce
15 ml/1 tbsp palm or light brown sugar
Finely grated zest and juice of 1 lime
Salt
2 kaffir lime leaves

700 g/1½ lb lean diced pork
1 bunch of spring onions (scallions), cut into short lengths
200 g/7 oz fresh baby spinach, well washed
4 tomatoes, quartered

TO SERVE:
Plain rice

1 Put the coconut milk, curry paste, fish sauce, sugar and lime zest and juice in a saucepan. Heat gently, stirring, until the oil rises to the surface and the mixture is very hot. Season to taste with salt.

2 Put the pork and spring onions in the crock pot and pour the hot coconut mixture over. Cover and cook on High for 3–4 hours or Low for 6–8 hours.

3 Stir in the spinach and tomatoes and cook on High or Low for a further 1 hour.

4 Serve spooned over rice.

This simple curry is delicious when served with accompaniments such as sliced banana tossed in lemon juice (to prevent browning), chopped onion, wedges of tomato, diced cucumber and mango chutney. You can substitute lamb for the pork and, if you like, use diced meat instead of chops. The curry powder can be either mild or hot, according to your taste.

English curried pork chops

SERVES 4

25 g/1 oz/2 tbsp butter
4 pork chops, trimmed of excess fat
1 large onion, chopped
1 eating (dessert) apple, peeled, cored and chopped
50 g/2 oz/⅓ cup sultanas (golden raisins)
30 ml/2 tbsp curry powder

60 ml/4 tbsp plain (all-purpose) flour
300 ml/½ pt/1¼ cups pork or beef stock
Salt and freshly ground black pepper
Desiccated (shredded) coconut to garnish

TO SERVE:
Plain rice

1 Heat half the butter in a pan, add the pork and brown on all sides. Transfer to the crock pot with a draining spoon.

2 Heat the remaining butter in the pan, add the onion and fry, stirring, for 2 minutes. Add the apple, sultanas and curry powder and fry for 30 seconds, stirring.

3 Stir in the flour, then remove the pan from the heat and blend in the stock. Return the pan to the heat and bring to the boil, stirring, until thickened (it will appear quite thick). Season to taste and pour over the pork. Cover and cook on High for 3 hours or Low for 6 hours.

4 Taste and re-season, if necessary. Serve sprinkled with desiccated coconut with rice, and the accompaniments suggested above.

The meat on these wonderful, saucy ribs simply melts in the mouth. I first had them with fresh pineapple but using canned is much easier. Should you wish to use fresh, you'll need to peel and dice it, removing any central core, and add about 120 ml/4 fl oz/½ cup of pineapple or orange juice to make up the liquid.

Thai chilli ribs with pineapple

SERVES 4

60 ml/4 tbsp plain (all-purpose) flour
Salt and freshly ground black pepper
60 ml/4 tbsp groundnut (peanut) oil
1.5 kg/3 lb pork spare ribs
500 g/18 oz/1 large can of
    pineapple chunks in natural juice
30 ml/2 tbsp light soy sauce
15 ml/1 tbsp tomato purée (paste)

30 ml/2 tbsp white wine vinegar
15 ml/1 tbsp palm or light brown
    sugar
1 red (bell) pepper, halved and thinly
    sliced
2 thin red chillies, seeded, if
    preferred, and thinly sliced

1 Mix the flour with a little salt and pepper and use to coat the ribs.

2 Heat the oil in a large frying pan, add the ribs a few at a time and fry until browned all over. Line the crock pot with non-stick baking parchment and place the ribs in it.

3 Drain the juice from the pineapple into the frying pan. Stir in the soy sauce, tomato purée, vinegar and sugar. Bring to the boil and pour over the ribs. Turn the ribs over so they are coated in the sauce.

4 Cover and cook on High for 3–4 hours or Low 6–8 hours. Ideally, re-arrange the ribs and turn them over half-way through cooking, so they all get an even coating of sauce.

5 Add the pineapple, sliced pepper and chillies, cover and cook for a further 1 hour on High until everything is tender and bathed in a sticky sauce. Serve hot.

Curried sausages may sound unusual, but this Anglo-Indian recipe makes a great supper dish and, surprisingly, is very tasty cold too! You can reduce the cooking time by cutting the potatoes into dice rather than chunks, but the very long cooking does give a delicious result. Use good-quality meaty, coarse-textured sausages with little or no added rusk.

Curried pork sausages with potatoes and beans

SERVES 4

200 g/7 oz French (green) beans
4 potatoes, cut into bite-sized
   chunks
450 g/1 lb thick pork sausages, cut
   into chunks
1 onion, chopped
1 large garlic clove, crushed
5 ml/1 tsp grated fresh root ginger
5 ml/1 tsp ground cumin
1.5 ml/¼ tsp hot chilli powder

1.5 ml/¼ tsp ground turmeric
5 ml/1 tsp garam masala
450 ml/¾ pt/2 cups passata (sieved
   tomatoes)
60 ml/4 tbsp boiling water
15 ml/1 tbsp mango chutney
2.5 ml/½ tsp salt

TO SERVE:
Chapattis

1   Top and tail the beans and cut them into short lengths. Put them in the crock pot and add the potatoes.

2   Heat a non-stick frying pan, add the sausage chunks and fry on all sides to brown. Transfer to the crock pot with a draining spoon.

3   Spoon off all but 15 ml/1 tbsp of the fat in the frying pan (you may not have any excess with very good-quality sausages). Add the onion to the pan and fry, stirring, for 2 minutes.

4   Stir all the remaining ingredients into the pan and bring to the boil. Transfer to the crock pot. Cover and cook on High for 4–5 hours or Low for 8–10 hours until the vegetables are really tender and everything is bathed in a thick sauce. Serve with chapattis.

This curry is simplicity itself to prepare. It is also delicious with two good handfuls of large raw peeled prawns thrown in for the last 30 minutes' cooking until they have just turned pink. Make sure they are thawed, if frozen, and well drained before adding them to the crock pot. Because this curry uses pork fillet, it doesn't take long to become tender and succulent.

Thai red pork curry

SERVES 4

400 ml/14 oz/1 large can of coconut milk
30 ml/2 tbsp Thai red curry paste
2 fat red chillies, seeded, if preferred, and cut into thin strips
5 ml/1 tsp palm or light brown sugar
2.5 ml/½ tsp salt

450 g/1 lb pork fillet, cut into 5 mm/¼ in thick slices
30 ml/2 tbsp chopped fresh coriander (cilantro)

TO SERVE:
Rice noodles

1   Heat the coconut milk in a pan with the curry paste, chillies, sugar and salt until boiling.

2   Lay the pork in the crock pot. Pour the sauce over, cover and cook on High for 2 hours or Low for 4 hours.

3   Serve spooned over rice noodles, sprinkled with the coriander.

Kidneys, especially pigs' kidneys, are an often forgotten treat. The soaking first takes away their strong flavour and they become beautifully tender cooked in the slow cooker. Use cultivated button mushrooms instead of shiitake, if you prefer. The sweet spicy sauce is excitingly different; experiment with the balance of soy and sweet chilli to suite your palate.

Sweet chillied kidneys with shiitake mushrooms

SERVES 4

450 g/1 lb pigs' kidneys
120 g/4½ oz shiitake mushrooms, sliced
30 ml/2 tbsp groundnut (peanut) oil
1 large onion, finely chopped
2 garlic cloves, crushed
60 ml/4 tbsp soy sauce

15 ml/1 tbsp sweet chilli sauce
30 ml/2 tbsp water
2 fat green chillies, seeded, if preferred, and thinly sliced

TO SERVE:
Plain rice

1 Halve the kidneys, remove and discard the cores, and soak in cold water for at least 1 hour. Drain and cut into chunks. Put in the crock pot with the mushrooms.

2 Heat the oil in a pan, add the onion and garlic and fry gently, stirring, for 2 minutes. Add the soy sauce, chilli sauce and water and stir until bubbling.

3 Stir in half the sliced chillies, then tip into the crock pot. Stir well, cover and cook on High for 2 hours or Low for 4 hours until the kidneys are tender but not hard and they are bathed in a rich sauce.

4 Serve spooned over plain boiled rice, garnished with the remaining sliced chilli.

If using a piece of pork shoulder, cutting it in half means more of the meat gets flavoured with the lovely spices and it is easier to shred after cooking. Belly pork is a flatter cut so has a larger surface area. This is a great dish to share with friends as you can make double the quantity in a large crock pot without having to increase the cooking time.

Pork and chilli burritos with apple and radish salsa

SERVES 4

10 ml/2 tsp cumin seeds, coarsely crushed
5 ml/1 tsp black peppercorns, coarsely crushed
5 ml/1 tsp crushed dried chillies
5 ml/1 tsp salt
700 g/1½ lb piece of pork shoulder, cut into 2 equal pieces, or lean belly pork, rinded and trimmed of excess fat
30 ml/2 tbsp groundnut (peanut) or sunflower oil
2 onions, roughly sliced
1 large garlic clove, crushed
200 ml/7 fl oz/scant 1 cup pork or beef stock
15 ml/1 tbsp tomato purée (paste)

8 flour tortillas
1 cos (romaine) lettuce, shredded
200 ml/7 fl oz/scant 1 cup soured (dairy sour) cream

FOR THE SALSA:
1 red apple, unpeeled, cut into small dice
4 spring onions (scallions), chopped
1 avocado, cut into small dice
8 radishes, chopped
1 fat red chilli, seeded, if preferred, and thinly sliced
Grated zest and juice of 1 lime
2.5 ml/½ tsp clear honey
15 ml/1 tbsp chopped fresh coriander (cilantro) or basil

1 Mix together the spices and salt. Make several slashes all over the pork and rub in the spice mixture.

2 Heat half the oil in a frying pan, add the pork and brown on all sides. Transfer to the crock pot with a draining spoon.

3 Heat the remaining oil, add the onions and brown quickly, stirring. Stir in the garlic, stock and tomato purée and bring to the boil. Pour over the meat, cover and cook on High for 4 hours or Low for 8 hours until really tender.

4 Lift the meat out of the pot and place it on a board. Shred with two forks, discarding excess fat.

5 Pour the liquid into a saucepan and boil rapidly until well reduced and thickened. Pour back into the crock pot, turn to Low, return the meat to the pot, stir, cover and leave until ready to serve.

6 Meanwhile, to make the salsa, mix together all the ingredients and place in a small bowl.

7 Heat the tortillas either between two plates over a pan of simmering water or briefly in the microwave.

8 When ready to serve, divide the meat mixture between the tortillas, top with the lettuce and a spoonful of soured cream. Fold up the bottoms, then shape into cones. Serve on plates with a little salsa spooned over.

This is a classic dish that is usually made by slow roasting in the oven but I love the moist tenderness of the pork when it is slow cooked instead, and you get more wonderfully concentrated juices too. It has all the flavours of the American Deep South and the rub – a mixture of heat and sweetness – is equally good for grilled or barbecued chicken.

Cajun-spiced pork loin

SERVES 4–6

FOR THE RUB:
2.5 ml/½ tsp salt
2.5 ml/½ tsp hot chilli powder
2.5 ml/½ tsp ground cumin
2.5 ml/½ tsp garlic granules
2.5 ml/½ tsp dried oregano
2.5 ml/½ tsp light brown sugar
1.5 ml/¼ tsp ground ginger
1.5 ml/¼ tsp ground allspice
Finely grated zest of ½ small lemon
Freshly ground black pepper

FOR THE PORK:
700 g/1½ lb piece of boned pork loin, rind removed

15 ml/1 tbsp groundnut (peanut) oil
4 potatoes, peeled and cut into chunks
200 ml/7 fl oz/scant 1 cup boiling pork or beef stock
Torn coriander (cilantro) leaves to garnish

TO SERVE:
Rolled flour tortillas and a mixed salad with sweetcorn kernels added

1 To make the rub, mix together all the ingredients, adding a good grinding of black pepper, and rub all over the pork loin.

2 Heat the oil in a frying pan, add the pork and brown on all sides. Place in the crock pot and put the frying pan aside for use later.

3 Arrange the potato chunks around the spiced pork and pour the boiling stock over. Cover and cook on High for 4 hours or Low for 8 hours until the pork is really tender.

4 When the pork is cooked, lift it out of the pot and place on a carving dish. Leave to stand for 10 minutes in a warm place.

5 Meanwhile, spoon off any excess fat from the pork cooking juices, then pour into the reserved frying pan. Bring to the boil, and boil rapidly for 2 minutes, stirring, until slightly thickened and reduced.

6 Carve the pork into thick slices, transfer to plates and spoon a little of the reduced cooking juices over. Serve, garnished with coriander, with rolled flour tortillas and a mixed salad with sweetcorn kernels.

For speed I've used a packet of stir-fry vegetables to serve with the pork, but if you have suitable fresh vegetables to hand, such as cabbage (finely shredded), carrots, peppers, celery, cucumber, courgettes (cut into matchsticks), onions and mushrooms (sliced), so much the better. Just stir-fry your selection of vegetables until they are very slightly softened.

Chinese red cooked pork and vegetables

SERVES 4

2.5 ml/½ tsp coriander seeds
5 ml/1 tsp cumin seeds
5 ml/1 tsp black peppercorns
2.5 cm/1 in piece fresh root ginger, grated
1 thin red chilli, seeded, if preferred, and chopped
2 garlic cloves, crushed
1 stalk of lemon grass, chopped
30 ml/2 tbsp groundnut (peanut) oil
10 ml/2 tsp rice vinegar
450 g/1 lb diced pork shoulder or leg

150 ml/¼ pt/⅔ cup water
30 ml/2 tbsp rice wine or dry sherry
30 ml/2 tbsp soy sauce, plus extra for sprinkling
1 onion, cut into wedges
1 piece of cinnamon stick
1 star anise
15 ml/1 tbsp cornflour (cornstarch)
350 g/12 oz packet of stir-fry vegetables
300 g/11 oz packet of fresh egg noodles

1 Using a pestle and mortar or a bowl and the end of a rolling pin, crush the seeds and peppercorns, then work in the ginger, chilli, garlic and lemon grass. Finally, work in half the oil and the vinegar to form a coarse, wet paste.

2 Put the pork in a sealable container, add the paste, mix well with the hands, cover and leave to marinate in the fridge for several hours or, preferably, overnight.

3 Put the pork in the crock pot. Put the water, rice wine or sherry, soy sauce, onion, cinnamon and star anise in a saucepan and bring to the boil. Pour over the pork, cover and cook on High for 3 hours or Low for 6 hours until really tender.

4 Discard the cinnamon and star anise. Pour the cooking liquid into a saucepan. Blend the cornflour with 15 ml/1 tbsp of water, stir in and bring to the boil. Cook for 1 minute, stirring, until thickened and clear, then pour back over the pork.

5 Heat the remaining oil in a wok or large frying pan, add the vegetables and stir-fry for 3 minutes. Add the noodles and toss until hot through. Sprinkle with soy sauce to taste and toss again.

6 Pile the vegetables and noodles into large warm bowls and spoon the pork and juices on top.

*The pork is slow cooked with onions and soy sauce, then tossed in spices
and returned to the pot with bamboo shoots and beansprouts. If you get it
all prepared in the morning and leave the pork to cook, it can be finished
off later in about an hour. Traditionally, the cooked pork is stir-fried with
the vegetables at the end – but my way saves washing up!*

Szechuan twice-cooked pork

SERVES 4–6

550 g/1¼ lb lean belly pork slices
1 onion, halved and thinly sliced
30 ml/2 tbsp soy sauce
150 ml/¼ pt/⅔ cup boiling water
2 garlic cloves, crushed
15 ml/1 tbsp black bean sauce
5 ml/1 tsp crushed dried chillies
15 ml/1 tbsp tomato purée (paste)
15 ml/1 tbsp hoisin sauce

15 ml/1 tbsp rice wine or dry sherry
225 g/8 oz/1 medium can of
   bamboo shoots, drained
200 g/7 oz/3½ cups fresh
   beansprouts
2 spring onions (scallions),
   shredded, to garnish

TO SERVE:
Plain rice or egg noodles

1   Put the pork in the crock pot with the onion, soy sauce and boiling
    water. Cover and cook on High for 3–4 hours or Low for 6–8 hours
    until really tender.

2   Lift the pork out of the pot, remove the rind and any bones, then
    cut the pork into chunky pieces.

3   Spoon off and discard any fat from the cooking liquid, pour into a
    saucepan and boil rapidly until reduced by half. Put back in the
    slow cooker and stir in all the flavourings, then the bamboo shoots
    and beansprouts. Stir until everything is coated in sauce, then top
    with the pork. Cover and cook on High for 45–60 minutes until the
    beansprouts are slightly softened and everything is piping hot.

4   Stir gently to incorporate the pork into the vegetables, then serve
    garnished with shredded spring onions with rice or egg noodles.

FISH
DISHES

Because fish cooks quickly it is easy to spoil it – whether frying, grilling or steaming. Cooking it in the slow cooker makes this a thing of the past and you won't have to stand over it any more. You can't, unfortunately, go out all day and leave it but, because the dishes take only a little preparation, you can pop one on to cook, then get ready for the meal at a leisurely pace – or even have a shower or a pre-dinner drink while it cooks.

Tandoori fish, prepared my way, is a delicate, soft creation and the crock pot cooks it beautifully. I have to admit I have never had this in India – I made up my version back in the 1970s and have adapted it for the slow cooker fairly recently. The sambal adds colour and flavour to what is essentially a light, summery dish. Any firm white fish will work in this recipe.

Tandoori fish with avocado and tomato sambal

SERVES 4

4 pieces of thick white fish fillet, about 150 g/5 oz each
150 ml/¼ pt/⅔ cup thick plain yoghurt
15 ml/1 tbsp lemon juice
5 ml/1 tsp ground cumin
5 ml/1 tsp ground coriander
5 ml/1 tsp paprika
2.5 ml/½ tsp ground turmeric
2.5 ml/½ tsp hot chilli powder
A good pinch of salt

FOR THE SAMBAL:
1 avocado, finely diced
1 small onion, finely chopped

1 fat green chilli, seeded, if preferred, and chopped
25 g/1 oz/3 tbsp sultanas (golden raisins)
2 tomatoes, seeded and chopped
Juice of ½ lime or lemon
15 ml/1 tbsp chopped fresh coriander (cilantro)
Freshly ground black pepper
A few torn fresh coriander leaves and wedges of lime or lemon to garnish

TO SERVE:
Pilau rice

1 Lay the fish in a shallow dish that will take it in one layer. Mix together the yoghurt, lemon juice, spices and salt and spoon over the fish. Turn the fish over in the mixture to coat completely, then leave to marinate for 2 hours in the fridge.

2 Transfer the fish with the marinade that is sticking to it to the crock pot, leaving behind any excess marinade. Cover and cook on Low for 1–1½ hours.

3 Meanwhile, to make the sambal, mix together all the ingredients, seasoning to taste with pepper. Spoon into a small dish and chill until ready to serve.

4 Transfer the fish to warm plates with a fish slice. Garnish with a few torn coriander leaves and wedges of lime or lemon and serve with the sambal and pilau rice.

This recipe comes from Trinidad but you'll find very similar dishes on many Caribbean islands. For a change from serving it with plain rice, try the curry spooned over couscous or quinoa and you will have an interesting variation of texture and flavour. Some versions have cubes of pineapple in it too, but I prefer the more subtle flavour of just the juice.

Caribbean prawn curry

SERVES 4

400 g/14 oz shelled raw king prawns (jumbo shrimp), thawed if frozen
30 ml/2 tbsp groundnut (peanut) oil
1 large onion, finely chopped
1 large garlic clove, finely chopped
2.5 cm/1 in piece of fresh root ginger, grated
5 ml/1 tsp ground cumin
5 ml/1 tsp ground coriander
5 ml/1 tsp ground turmeric
2.5 ml/½ tsp crushed dried chillies
10 ml/2 tsp black mustard seeds

1 beefsteak tomato, skinned and chopped
10 ml/2 tsp tomato purée (paste)
150 ml/¼ pt/⅔ cup pineapple juice
Salt and freshly ground black pepper
Juice of ½ lime
15 ml/1 tbsp chopped fresh coriander (cilantro)
A few torn coriander leaves and wedges of lime to garnish

TO SERVE:
Plain rice

1 Using the sharp point of a knife, make a slit down the back of each prawn (this is so they 'butterfly' when cooked). Remove the black vein, if necessary. Place in the crock pot.

2 Heat the oil in a saucepan, add the onion and fry, stirring, for 2 minutes until softened but not browned. Add the garlic and spices and fry, stirring, until the mustard seeds start to 'pop'.

3 Add the tomato, tomatoe purée, pineapple juice and seasoning to taste. Bring to the boil and pour over the prawns. Cover and cook on Low for 1 hour.

4 Add the lime juice and coriander, taste and re-season if necessary. Spoon over rice, garnish with a few torn coriander leaves and some wedges of lime and serve hot.

This pilaf is very easy to make as the entire dish is cooked in the crock pot and no other accompaniment is necessary, except perhaps a crisp green salad if you like. For a stunning summer dish, leave it to get cold, pack it into small pots, then turn them out on to beds of lettuce and serve with a dressing made from a blend of mayonnaise and French dressing.

Tobago curried crab pilaf

SERVES 4

350 g/12 oz/1½ cups long-grain rice
15 g/½ oz/1 tbsp butter
15 ml/1 tbsp groundnut (peanut) oil
1 bunch of spring onions (scallions), chopped
1 garlic clove, chopped
1 fat red chilli, seeded, if preferred, and chopped

15 ml/1 tbsp curry powder
2 x 170 g/6 oz/small cans of white crabmeat
400 g/14 oz/1 large can of coconut milk
Juice of ½ lime
Salt and freshly ground black pepper
Lime wedges to garnish

1 Wash the rice well in a sieve (strainer) and drain thoroughly.

2 Heat the butter and oil in a saucepan. Reserve 15 ml/1 tbsp of the green chopped spring onion for garnish, add the remainder to the pan with the garlic and chilli and fry, stirring, for 1 minute.

3 Add the curry powder and rice and stir for a further 1 minute. Tip into the crock pot.

4 Drain the liquor from the cans of crab into a measuring jug and put the meat on top of the rice mixture.

5 Pour the coconut milk and lime juice into the measuring jug and make up to 900 ml/1½ pts/3¾ cups with water. Pour into the pan and season with a little salt and pepper. Bring to the boil, stirring, and tip into the crock pot. Stir, cover and cook on Low for 2 hours until the rice is just tender and has absorbed the liquid.

6 Fluff up with a fork and season to taste. Serve garnished with the lime wedges.

I first had this in a restaurant in England and loved it so much I had to re-create it for this book. It takes only minutes to prepare but it's definitely worth bothering to blanch the vegetables as this helps them retain their colour and it ensures they cook in the same time as the fish. Pollock is a good alternative to cod but any other firm white fish fillet will be just as good.

Thai green fish curry with broccoli and beans

SERVES 4

225 g/8 oz broccoli, cut into small florets

100 g/4 oz French (green) beans, topped, tailed and cut into short lengths

1 fat green chilli, seeded and cut into thin strips

4 cod or other white fish fillets, about 150 g/5 oz each, skinned and cut into large chunks

400 g/14 oz/1 large can of coconut milk

30 ml/2 tbsp Thai green curry paste

Salt and freshly ground black pepper

A few torn coriander (cilantro) leaves to garnish

TO SERVE:
Jasmine rice

1 Blanch the broccoli and beans in boiling water for 3 minutes and drain. Place in the crock pot with the chilli strips and fish.

2 Bring the coconut milk and curry paste to the boil in a saucepan, then pour over the fish and vegetables. Season lightly. Cover and cook on Low for 1½ hours until everything is tender.

3 Taste and re-season if necessary. Serve spooned over jasmine rice in bowls, garnished with a few torn coriander leaves.

I first had this with fresh pineapple but, as it's crushed up anyway, a can of pineapple in natural juice works equally well and saves a lot of work. I prefer to use salt cod fillet but, if you buy it with the bone in, chop it into pieces, bone and all. If it has the bone, you may need a greater quantity than I give here, particularly for those with big appetites.

Eurasian salt cod and pineapple curry

SERVES 4

450 g/1 lb salt cod fillet
1 onion, roughly chopped
2 thin red chillies, seeded, if preferred
1 stalk of lemon grass, roughly chopped
1 garlic clove, roughly chopped
15 ml/1 tablespoon Thai fish sauce
10 ml/2 tsp grated fresh root ginger or galangal
30 ml/2 tbsp groundnut (peanut) or vegetable oil

1 red (bell) pepper, cut into small diamond shapes
430 g/15 oz/1 large can of crushed pineapple in natural juice
400 g/14 oz/1 large can of extra-thick coconut milk
Salt and freshly ground black pepper

TO SERVE:
Rice noodles

1 Soak the fish in cold water for at least 12 hours or overnight, changing the water twice. Drain, remove the skin and cut the flesh into large chunks.

2 Using either a hand blender or a pestle and mortar, pound the onion, chillies, lemon grass, garlic, fish sauce and ginger or galangal to a coarse paste.

3 Heat the oil in a pan, add the paste and fry, stirring, for 3 minutes.

4 Add the pepper diamonds, pineapple and juice and the coconut milk and bring to the boil, stirring.

5 Put the fish in the crock pot and pour the pineapple mixture over. Cover and cook on Low for 2 hours until the fish is tender.

6 Taste and season as necessary. Serve the curry with rice noodles – no other accompaniment is necessary.

This curry is really more of a delicious soup! In fact you could serve it as such but it's more often spooned over lots of plain boiled rice to help soak up all the glorious liquid flavoured with an enticing combination of spices. I find that even coley – far too often considered to be the poor relation of white fish – is fine for this dish and is very economical too.

East African curried fish stew

SERVES 4

550 g/1¼ lb thick white fish fillet, cut into large chunks
Salt and freshly ground black pepper
30 ml/2 tbsp groundnut (peanut) oil
1 onion, halved and thinly sliced
2 garlic cloves, crushed
10 ml/2 tsp black mustard seeds
5 ml/1 tsp crushed dried red chillies
5 ml/1 tsp ground cumin
5 ml/1 tsp ground coriander
1.5 ml/¼ tsp ground turmeric
Juice of 1 lime
5 ml/1 tsp tamarind paste
1 red (bell) pepper, thinly sliced

1 fat red chilli, seeded, if preferred, and thinly sliced
400 g/14 oz/1 large can of chopped tomatoes
400 g/14 oz/1 large can of coconut milk
150 ml/¼ pt/⅔ cup fish or chicken stock
A few torn fresh coriander (cilantro) leaves to garnish

TO SERVE:
Plain rice

1 Season the fish with salt and pepper and place in the crock pot.

2 Heat the oil in the pan, add the onion and garlic and fry for 3 minutes, stirring, until lightly golden. Stir in all the spices, the lime juice and tamarind paste and fry for 1 minute.

3 Add the pepper slices, chilli, tomatoes, coconut milk and stock. Bring to the boil and add salt and pepper to taste. Pour over the fish, cover and cook on Low for 1 hour.

4 Taste and re-season, if necessary. Serve spooned over rice in large soup bowls. Garnish with a few torn coriander leaves and eat with a spoon.

Slow-cooked chunks of salmon in spices and coconut milk makes a beautifully moist, flavoursome dish. It's important that the lime juice is not added to the crock pot but is squeezed over the finished dish, just before serving, to cut through the richness. Serve it with a fresh and crunchy watercress and cucumber salad for another wonderful flavour sensation.

Sri Lankan chilli salmon stew

SERVES 4

15 g/½ oz/1 tbsp ghee or butter
2 onions, roughly chopped
550 g/1¼ lb salmon fillet, skinned
  and cut into chunks
2.5 ml/½ tsp crushed dried chillies
1.5 ml/¼ tsp ground turmeric
2.5 ml/½ tsp ground cumin
30 ml/2 tbsp tomato purée (paste)

400 g/14 oz/1 large can of thick
  coconut milk
Salt and freshly ground black pepper
1 lime

TO SERVE:
Jasmine rice and a watercress and
  cucumber salad

1   Heat the ghee or butter in a pan, add the onions and fry gently, stirring, for about 4 minutes until soft and golden. Transfer to the crock pot with a draining spoon. Add the salmon to the crock pot.

2   Add the spices to the pan and fry, stirring, for 30 seconds. Blend in the tomato purée and coconut milk and season to taste. Bring to the boil, stirring, then pour over the fish. Cover and cook on Low for 1 hour.

3   Meanwhile, thinly pare the zest from the lime and cut it into thin shreds. Boil in water for 2 minutes, drain, rinse with cold water and drain again. Squeeze the lime juice.

4   When the fish is cooked, add lime juice to taste, garnish with the lime zest and serve with jasmine rice and a watercress and cucumber salad.

*Slow cooking squid in olive oil with fresh chillies and lime renders it
beautifully tender, sweet and succulent. This weight would be at least 16
baby squid – enough for a delicious light lunch for four, but it would also
serve eight as a small starter. You can buy large, thick squid rings instead
of baby squid and cook them in the same way if you prefer.*

Squid in chilli sauce

SERVES 4

450 g/1 lb cleaned baby squid, split
  open and tentacles trimmed
120 ml/4 fl oz/½ cup olive oil
1 bunch of spring onions (scallions),
  chopped
1 garlic clove, crushed
1 thin green chilli, seeded,
  if preferred, and chopped
1 thin red chilli, seeded, if preferred,
  and chopped

Finely grated zest and juice of 1 lime
Salt and freshly ground black pepper
5 cm/2 in piece of cucumber, finely
  diced
30 ml/2 tbsp chopped fresh parsley
  to garnish

TO SERVE:
Crusty bread and a crisp green salad

1 Lay the squid in the crock pot.

2 Blend together all the remaining ingredients except the cucumber.
Pour over the squid, cover and cook on Low for 2 hours.

3 Stir in the cucumber, taste and re-season if necessary. Sprinkle
with the parsley and serve with crusty bread to mop up the juices
and a crisp green salad.

This is named after the town in the Gulf of Mexico where it originated. Although I specify red snapper in the ingredients, and it does look spectacular, in fact you can experiment with any whole fish. You get so many flavour sensations with this dish – sweet, salty, hot and sharp – that really simple accompaniments are all that are needed to complement it perfectly.

Fish Veracruz-style with chillies, caperberries and olives

SERVES 4

4 red snapper, cleaned and scaled
Finely grated zest and juice of 1 lime
2.5 ml/½ tsp salt
Freshly ground black pepper
1 thin red chilli, seeded, if preferred, and finely chopped
30 ml/2 tbsp olive oil
2 onions, thinly sliced
2 garlic cloves, crushed
1 green (bell) pepper, cut into diamond shapes

700 g/1½ lb ripe tomatoes, quartered
5 ml/1 tsp caster (superfine) sugar
8 slices of pickled jalapeno pepper, from a jar
25 g/1 oz pickled caperberries
50 g/2 oz/⅓ cup stuffed green olives
Wedges of lime to garnish

TO SERVE:
Plain boiled potatoes and a cucumber salad

1 Rinse the red snapper and pat them dry with kitchen paper (paper towels). Make several slashes on both sides of the flesh and rub with the lime zest and juice, the salt, a good grinding of pepper and the chilli.

2 Heat the oil in a frying pan. Add the onions, garlic and pepper diamonds and cook, stirring, for 3 minutes.

3 Add all the remaining ingredients and cook for a further 3 minutes. Spoon into the crock pot and top with the red snapper in a single layer. Cover and cook on Low for 1½ hours or until the fish flakes easily with a fork and the tomatoes are cooked but still hold their shape.

4 Transfer the fish to warm plates and spoon the tomato mixture around. Garnish with wedges of lime and serve with potatoes and a cucumber salad.

VEGETABLE
DISHES

All these dishes can be eaten on their own or served as a side dish with some simply cooked meat, chicken or fish. Vegetables are often complemented by the use of spices, whether you want a mixed vegetable curry or some lovely spiced sweetcorn cobs. Slow cooking ensures you retain nearly all their nutrients as you always serve them in the cooking juices and, in addition, they don't fall apart so easily as they cook so gently.

This is often served with meat or chicken Indian-type curries. Ring the changes with any vegetables you have to hand. If you have a large crock pot, you can make this and a meat curry in two bowls side by side in the cooker, with about 2.5 cm/1 in of boiling water in the crock pot. This curry is also good with eggs or paneer – and satisfying on its own.

Mixed vegetable curry

SERVES 4

25 g/1 oz/2 tbsp ghee or butter
1 large onion, chopped
1 large garlic clove, crushed
10 ml/2 tsp cumin seeds
5 ml/1 tsp ground turmeric
15 ml/1 tbsp garam masala
175 g/6 oz creamed coconut
600 ml/1 pt/2½ cups water
30 ml/2 tbsp tomato purée (paste)
5 ml/1 tsp salt
Juice of 1 lime

1 large carrot, sliced
1 aubergine (eggplant), diced
1 green (bell) pepper, diced
1 red pepper, diced
1 large potato, diced
1 small head of cauliflower, cut into
   florets
100 g/4 oz frozen green beans,
   thawed
1 bay leaf

1   Heat the ghee or butter in a saucepan, add the onion and garlic and fry, stirring, for 2 minutes.

2   Add the spices and fry for 30 seconds. Stir in the coconut, water and tomato purée and bring to the boil, stirring, until the coconut has melted. Stir in the salt and lime juice.

3   Put all the vegetables in the crock pot and pour the sauce over. Add the bay leaf. Cover and cook on High for 3 hours or Low for 6 hours until the vegetables are tender.

4   Taste and re-season, if necessary. Remove and discard the bay leaf before serving.

I love this as an accompaniment to a meat or chicken curry but it's great with plain grilled meat, poultry or fish too. You can also roughly crush it with a fork when cooked and spoon it on to coriander and garlic naan breads or chapattis for a light lunch or supper dish. When pumpkin isn't available, you can use any other orange-fleshed squashes instead.

South Indian pumpkin

SERVES 4

30 ml/2 tbsp groundnut (peanut) oil
1 large onion, halved and thinly
   sliced
30 ml/2 tbsp black mustard seeds
2.5 ml/½ tsp ground turmeric
5 ml/1 tsp ground cumin
5 ml/1 tsp ground coriander
5 ml/1 tsp hot chilli powder

5 ml/1 tsp garam masala
2.5 ml/½ tsp salt
5 ml/1 tsp palm or light brown sugar
150 ml/¼ pt/⅔ cup water
1 small pumpkin, about 700 g/1½ lb,
   peeled, seeded and cut into bite-
   sized chunks
2 small bay leaves

1 Heat the oil in a frying pan, add the onion and fry, stirring, for 4 minutes until lightly golden. Stir in the mustard seeds and cook until they start to 'pop'.

2 Add the remaining spices and stir for 30 seconds. Add the salt, sugar and water and bring to the boil.

3 Put the pumpkin in the crock pot with the bay leaves and pour the spicy sauce over. Cover and cook on High for 2 hours or Low for 4 hours until tender.

4 Remove and discard the bay leaves, stir gently and serve. No garnish is needed.

If you like a stronger mushroom flavour, use large open or field mushrooms and cut them into chunks. It is delicious on its own as a light lunch with some rice or chapattis or serve it as a vegetable accompaniment to meat or chicken. It goes particularly well with tandoori fish too. Serve this curry on boiled basmati rice to make a complete meal.

Mushroom and pea curry with almonds

SERVES 4

20 g/¾ oz/1½ tbsp ghee or butter
5 ml/1 tsp cumin seeds
5 ml/1 tsp sesame seeds
5 ml/1 tsp black mustard seeds
1 large onion, chopped
2 garlic cloves, crushed
2.5 cm/1 in piece of fresh root ginger, grated
350 g/12 oz button mushrooms
30 ml/2 tbsp mild curry paste

400 g/14 oz/1 large can of chopped tomatoes
Salt and freshly ground black pepper
50 g/2 oz/½ cup frozen peas, thawed
30 ml/2 tbsp chopped fresh coriander (cilantro)
25 g/1 oz/¼ cup toasted flaked (shredded) almonds

1   Melt the ghee or butter in a large pan. Add the seeds and fry until they start to 'pop'.

2   Add the onion and garlic and fry, stirring, for 2 minutes. Stir in the ginger and mushrooms, then tip into the crock pot.

3   Add the curry paste to the pan and fry, stirring, for 1 minute. Stir in the tomatoes, bring to the boil and pour over the mushrooms. Season with salt and pepper. Cover and cook on High for 2 hours or Low for 4 hours until the mushrooms are really tender.

4   Add the peas and cook for a further 3–4 minutes or until they are hot through but still bright green.

5   Taste and re-season, if necessary, then serve with the coriander and almonds scattered over.

Gobi aloo is a popular dish in Northern India where it is usually served as an accompaniment to a main course, but I like it with some paneer (Indian cheese) stirred in at the end for a light lunch dish – but this is my own idea and certainly isn't traditional! Any leftovers can be blended with stock for a great, smooth curried cauliflower soup.

Cauliflower and potato curry

SERVES 4

30 ml/2 tbsp groundnut (peanut) oil
5 ml/1 tsp cumin seeds
2.5 ml/½ tsp coriander seeds, lightly crushed
1 large onion, halved and thinly sliced
2.5 ml/½ tsp ground turmeric
5 ml/1 tsp grated fresh root ginger
2 fat green chillies, seeded, if preferred, and finely chopped
1 large garlic clove, crushed

1 beefsteak tomato, skinned and chopped
5 ml/1 tsp caster (superfine) sugar
2 large potatoes, peeled and cut into walnut-sized pieces
1 small cauliflower, cut into florets
150 ml/¼ pt/⅔ cup boiling water
Salt and freshly ground black pepper
A few torn fresh coriander (cilantro) leaves to garnish

1 Heat the oil in a large saucepan, add the cumin and coriander seeds and fry until they begin to sizzle. Add the onion and fry, stirring, for 3 minutes.

2 Add the remaining spices, the garlic, tomato and sugar and stir for 1 minute.

3 Add the potatoes and cauliflower and stir until coated in the mixture. Stir in the boiling water and seasoning to taste.

4 Tip into the crock pot, cover and cook on High for 3 hours or Low for 6 hours until really tender.

5 Stir gently, then serve garnished with a few torn coriander leaves.

Traditionally these are prepared by frying slowly in oil for all the cooking time but I find they can stick to the pan. By transferring them to the crock pot, they cook perfectly with no stirring and no sticking. You use far less oil too, which has to be another advantage. They are so delicious, I usually make twice the quantity as I can't resist nibbling them cold!

Bombay potatoes with tomatoes

SERVES 4

30 ml/2 tbsp groundnut (peanut) oil
2 fat green chillies, seeded, if
    preferred, and finely chopped
5 ml/1 tsp ground cumin
5 ml/1 tsp ground coriander
1.5 ml/¼ tsp ground turmeric
1 beefsteak tomato, skinned and
    chopped

60 ml/4 tbsp boiling water
700 g/1½ lb potatoes, peeled and
    cut into walnut-sized pieces
Salt and freshly ground black pepper
30 ml/2 tbsp chopped fresh
    coriander (cilantro)

1   Heat the oil in a pan, add the spices and fry, stirring, for
    30 seconds. Add the tomato and bring to the boil, stirring. Add the
    boiling water.

2   Put the potatoes in the crock pot. Add the tomato mixture, season
    well with salt and pepper and stir thoroughly.

3   Cover and cook on High for 3 hours or Low for 6 hours until the
    potatoes are really tender.

4   Taste and re-season, if necessary. Sprinkle with the coriander and
    serve hot.

You can cook the cobs in plain butter or a herb-flavoured sauce in the slow cooker to enjoy when you're not in a spicy mood – but the flavour of the butter and the curry paste in this recipe is fantastic. Try them as a starter or serve them as an accompaniment to grilled meat, poultry or fish. If you like more fire, use a hot curry paste instead of mild.

Corn cobs in curried butter sauce

SERVES 4

50 g/2 oz/¼ cup butter, cut into
  small pieces
30 ml/2 tbsp mild curry paste

120 ml/4 fl oz/½ cup boiling water
4 corn cobs, thawed, if frozen, and
  halved

1 Put the butter in the crock pot and cook on High for 30 minutes until melted.

2 Stir in the curry paste and water, then add the corn cobs. Turn so they are coated in the curry butter. Cover and cook on High for 3 hours or Low for 6 hours until a kernel comes away from the cob easily with a fork. Ideally, turn the cobs over once half-way through cooking.

3 Serve hot with the curry sauce spooned over.

You can cook 100 g/4 oz/⅔ cup of dried red kidney beans in the slow cooker first (following the instructions for Chilli Beans and Vegetables on page 118), instead of adding the drained canned beans. Serve the chilli spooned over plain boiled rice or as a filling for flour tortillas or crisp corn tacos, as you would a meat-based chilli.

Aubergine and sweet potato chilli

SERVES 4

30 ml/2 tbsp groundnut (peanut) oil
1 large onion, halved and sliced
1 large garlic clove, crushed
2.5 ml/½ tsp hot chilli powder (or to taste)
5 ml/1 tsp ground cumin
1 piece of cinnamon stick
1 bay leaf
400 g/14 oz/1 large can of chopped tomatoes
2.5 ml/½ tsp caster (superfine) sugar

Salt and freshly ground black pepper
1 large aubergine (eggplant), diced
1 sweet potato, diced
2 x 400 g/14 oz/large cans of red kidney beans, drained
30 ml/2 tbsp chopped fresh coriander (cilantro)
Soured (dairy sour) cream to garnish

TO SERVE:
Grated Cheddar or Montery Jack cheese

1 Heat the oil in a pan, add the onion and garlic and fry, stirring, for 2 minutes. Add the spices, bay leaf, tomatoes, sugar and some salt and pepper and bring to the boil, stirring.

2 Put the aubergine, sweet potato and kidney beans in the crock pot, then pour the sauce over. Stir well, cover and cook on High for 3 hours or Low for 6 hours until the vegetables are tender.

3 Taste the chilli and re-season, if necessary. Discard the cinnamon stick and bay leaf. Stir in half the coriander and serve garnished with a spoonful of soured cream and the remaining coriander, and grated cheese handed separately.

This is also really good with cubes of Feta cheese stirred in at the end instead of the paneer. You can cook the courgettes without browning them first, if you prefer, but the flavour won't be so intense. Try this with two or three medium-sized aubergines instead of the courgettes for a change, too. If you like a lot of heat, double the crushed chillies to 5 ml/1 tsp.

Spiced courgettes with paneer

SERVES 4

45 ml/3 tbsp groundnut (peanut) oil
4 large courgettes (zucchini), sliced
1 onion, finely chopped
1.5 ml/¼ tsp asafoetida
5 ml/1 tsp ground cumin
2.5 ml/½ tsp crushed dried chillies
450 ml/¾ pt/2 cups passata (sieved tomatoes)

2.5 ml/½ tsp caster (superfine) sugar
1.5 ml/¼ tsp gram masala
100 g/4 oz paneer, cut into small dice

TO SERVE:
Basmati rice

1 Heat the oil in a pan, add the courgettes and fry until golden on both sides. Transfer to the crock pot with a draining spoon.

2 Add the onion and spices to the pan and fry for 1 minute. Stir in the passata and sugar and bring to the boil.

3 Pour the tomato mixture over the courgettes, cover and cook on High for 1½–2 hours or Low for 3–4 hours until tender and bathed in sauce.

4 Stir in the garam masala and paneer, cover and cook for a further 5 minutes. Serve hot with basmati rice.

This is a lovely accompaniment to any fairly plain meat, chicken or fish dish. I particularly like it with grilled lamb steaks or chops. You could experiment with other root vegetables, such as swede, parsnips or Jerusalem artichokes, and try using chopped fresh basil instead of mint. For added colour, add a large thickly sliced carrot with the turnips.

Braised spiced turnips with tomatoes and mint

SERVES 4

30 ml/2 tbsp groundnut (peanut) oil
4 ripe tomatoes, skinned and
   chopped
5 ml/1 tsp palm or light brown sugar
5 ml/1 tsp paprika
2.5 ml/½ tsp ground cumin
2.5 ml/½ tsp ground cinnamon

1.5 ml/¼ tsp hot chilli powder
60 ml/4 tbsp water
4 large turnips, cut into bite-sized
   pieces
Salt and freshly ground black pepper
60 ml/4 tbsp chopped fresh mint
30 ml/2 tbsp thick plain yoghurt

1 Heat the oil in a saucepan, add the tomatoes and fry, stirring, for about 3 minutes until pulpy. Stir in the sugar, spices and water.

2 Put the turnips in the crock pot. Add the hot sauce, season well, cover and cook on High for 3 hours or Low for 6 hours until the turnips are really tender and bathed in sauce.

3 Taste and re-season if necessary. Stir in half the mint and serve topped with the yoghurt and the remaining mint.

This is a delicious dish on its own with crusty bread or pittas or served with any grilled meat or chicken. Any leftover beetroot can be chopped, mixed with a splash of white balsamic condiment and served as a relish with cold meats. For added sweetness, throw a handful of raisins into the crock pot with the beetroot.

Spiced beetroot with raita

SERVES 4

30 ml/2 tbsp groundnut (peanut) oil
5 ml/1 tsp cumin seeds
1 large onion, chopped
1 large garlic clove, crushed
15 ml/1 tbsp plain (all-purpose) flour
2.5 ml/½ tsp hot chilli powder
1.5 ml/¼ tsp asafoetida
2 tomatoes, skinned and chopped
5 ml/1 tsp tomato purée (paste)
10 ml/2 tsp mango chutney

150 ml/¼ pt/⅔ cup vegetable stock
4 raw beetroot (red beets), peeled
 and cut into chunks

FOR THE RAITA:
150 ml/¼ pt/⅔ cup thick plain
 yoghurt
5 cm/2 in piece of cucumber, grated
5 ml/1 tsp dried mint
Freshly ground black pepper

1 Heat the oil, add the cumin seeds and fry for 30 seconds. Add the onion and three-quarters of the garlic and fry for 2 minutes, stirring.

2 Blend in the flour, chilli powder, asafoetida, tomatoes, tomato purée, chutney and stock and bring to the boil, stirring.

3 Put the beetroot in the crock pot and pour the sauce over. Cover and cook on High for 3 hours or Low for 6 hours until tender and bathed in sauce.

4 Meanwhile, to make the raita, put the yoghurt in a small bowl. Squeeze the cucumber to remove excess moisture, then stir into the yoghurt with the remaining garlic, the mint and pepper to taste. Chill until ready to serve.

5 Spoon the beetroot into a serving dish and top with a little of the raita. Serve the rest handed separately.

Sag aloo is a popular side dish to serve with meat curries. But it also makes a great main course, with some poached or fried eggs and fried tomatoes. You could even shape 'wells' in the cooked spinach mixture with the back of a spoon, break eggs into them, then cover and cook on Low for 20 minutes or so until the eggs are set to your liking.

Mild spinach and potato curry with green pepper

SERVES 4

500 g/18 oz frozen leaf spinach, thawed
60 ml/4 tbsp groundnut (peanut) oil
15 ml/1 tbsp black mustard seeds
5 ml/1 tsp cumin seeds
1 large onion, halved and thinly sliced
1 large garlic clove, crushed
A pinch of asafoetida

2 large potatoes, peeled and cut into dice
1 green (bell) pepper, cut into chunks
A good pinch of hot chilli powder
120 ml/4 fl oz/½ cup water
Salt to taste
2 tomatoes, quartered

1 Squeeze the spinach well to remove as much of the excess moisture as you can. Place in the crock pot.

2 Heat the oil in a large saucepan, add the mustard and cumin seeds and fry until they start to 'pop'. Add the onion and garlic and fry, stirring, for 2 minutes.

3 Add all the remaining ingredients except the tomatoes. Bring to the boil, then tip into the crock pot. Cover and cook on High for 2–3 hours or Low for 4–6 hours until the potatoes are tender.

4 Add the tomatoes and cook for a further 30 minutes.

PULSES AND GRAIN-BASED
DISHES

Here I've included everything from various dhals – lentil curries – to rice and other grain dishes, like my quinoa and barley pilafs, chick pea and dried bean recipes and a tofu (bean curd) one. The slow cooker can be used to cook soaked dried pulses before adding the other ingredients or, if you prefer, you can used canned ones and start the recipe at the appropriate point in the recipe.

You'll find this lentil dish on Indian restaurant and take-away menus as masoor dhal. It's the ideal accompanaiment to serve with grills, tandoori dishes or kebabs. As lentils contain vegetable protein, try adding some cubes of cheddar cheese just before serving with some naan breads. Or it's also good served with rice and salad for a light veggie supper or lunch.

Red lentil curry

SERVES 4

175 g/6 oz/1 cup red lentils
1 onion, finely chopped
5 ml/1 tsp ground turmeric
5 ml/1 tsp grated fresh root ginger
450 ml/¾ pint/2 cups boiling water
40 g/1½ oz/3 tbsp ghee or butter
5 ml/1 tsp cumin seeds

5 ml/1 tsp ground coriander
10 ml/2 tsp paprika
1.5 ml/¼ tsp hot chilli powder
A pinch of asafoetida
15 ml/1 tbsp chopped fresh
  coriander (cilantro) to garnish

1 Put the lentils in the crock pot with the onion, turmeric and ginger. Add the water, stir well, cover and cook on High for 1½–2 hours or Low for 3–4 hours until pulpy and most of the liquid has been absorbed.

2 When the dhal is ready, heat the ghee or butter in a small pan, add the cumin seeds and fry until they sizzle. Stir all in the remaining ingredients. Pour into the cooked lentils and stir to mix. Garnish with the coriander and serve hot.

This isn't one to be left all day because even in the slow cooker it takes just an hour. It does make a really tasty dish, though, served on its own or as an accompaniment to grilled chicken or kebabs. Quinoa (pronounced kee-nwa) is the seeds of the goosefoot grass. The Incas held it to be a sacred crop and it's said the emperor sowed the seeds with golden tools!

Peanut quinoa pilaf with chilli and coriander

SERVES 4

175 g/6 oz/1 cup quinoa
45 ml/3 tbsp smooth peanut butter
600 ml/1 pt/2½ cups boiling chicken
  or vegetable stock
2 fat red chillies, seeded, if
  preferred, and finely chopped
Finely grated zest and juice of 1 lime

2 spring onions (scallions), finely
  chopped
30 ml/2 tbsp fresh coriander
  (cilantro), chopped
30 ml/2 tbsp chopped fresh parsley
Salt and freshly ground black pepper
Wedges of lime to garnish

1 Rinse the quinoa and drain well, then put in the crock pot.

2 Blend the peanut butter with the stock, chillies and lime zest and juice and add to the pot. Stir well, cover and cook on Low for 1 hour until tender and the quinoa has absorbed all the stock.

3 Stir in the spring onions, herbs and seasoning to taste. Garnish with lime wedges and serve.

Barley cooks wonderfully in the slow cooker and retains its nutty texture. Here it's steeped in a mild curry and coconut stock and then prawns are added for the last few minutes so they retain their succulence. I like to serve it in open soup plates with some crusty bread and a crisp green salad. Don't forget that frozen foods must be completely thawed before going in the crock pot.

Curried barley and prawn pilaf

SERVES 4

15 g/½ oz/1 tbsp ghee or butter
15 ml/1 tbsp groundnut (peanut) or
   sunflower oil
1 bunch of spring onions (scallions),
   chopped
1 garlic clove, crushed
1 red (bell) pepper, diced
5 ml/1 tsp ground turmeric
10 ml/2 tsp mild curry paste
200 g/7 oz/1 cup pearl barley

400 g/14 oz/1 large can of coconut
   milk
300 ml/½ pt/1¼ cups chicken stock
1 bay leaf
100 g/4 oz/1 cup frozen peas,
   thawed
400 g/14 oz raw peeled king prawns
   (jumbo shrimp), thawed if frozen
Salt and freshly ground black pepper
30 ml/2 tbsp chopped fresh parsley
   and wedges of lime to garnish

1 Heat the ghee or butter and oil in a pan, add the spring onions, garlic and diced pepper and fry, stirring, for 1 minute.

2 Stir in the turmeric and curry paste and cook for a further 30 seconds. Stir in the barley until the grains are glistening, then add the coconut milk, stock and bay leaf. Bring to the boil and tip everything into the crock pot.

3 Cover and cook on High for 2–3 hours or Low for 4–6 hours, stirring in the peas and prawns 15 minutes before you want to serve (the prawns are cooked when they turn pink).

4 Season to taste and serve garnished with the chopped parsley and wedges of lime.

The eggs take on a creamy quality when slow-cooked – not hard and rubbery, though you might expect this. Here they are married with rustic chick peas and bathed in a creamy coconut sauce flavoured with spices and fresh coriander. Because this is an egg dish, the Low setting must be used, though it will sit quite happily for another hour if necessary.

Curried eggs with chick peas

SERVES 4

1 onion, grated
1 garlic clove, crushed
2.5 cm/1 in piece of fresh root ginger, grated
15 ml/1 tbsp groundnut (peanut) oil
5 ml/1 tsp ground coriander
5 ml/1 tsp ground cumin
5 ml/1 tsp garam masala
2.5 ml/½ tsp ground turmeric
2.5 ml/½ tsp hot chilli powder
300 ml/½ pt/1¼ cups boiling water
50 g/2 oz creamed coconut
Salt

15 ml/1 tbsp chopped fresh coriander (cilantro)
8 hard boiled (hard-cooked) eggs, shelled
2 x 435 g/15 oz/large cans of chick peas (garbanzos), drained
A few torn coriander leaves to garnish

TO SERVE:
Naan breads, a green salad and mango chutney

1 Mix the onion, garlic, ginger, oil and ground spices to a paste. Heat a frying pan, add the paste and fry, stirring, for 1 minute.

2 Stir in the water and creamed coconut and stir until the coconut melts and the sauce is thick. Season with salt and stir in the chopped coriander.

3 Put the eggs and chick peas in the crock pot. Spoon the sauce over, cover and cook on Low for 2–3 hours.

4 Serve hot garnished with torn coriander leaves with naan breads, a green salad and chutney.

For added flavour, you could use smoked tofu instead of plain. But if you aren't keen on tofu at all, do try this mild curry anyway but using paneer, the Indian bland firm cheese, which is also suitable for vegetarians. If you prefer hard-cooked eggs rather than soft, simply add them to the crock pot and cook them for about 30 minutes instead of 20 minutes.

Tofu and egg curry

SERVES 4

30 ml/2 tbsp groundnut (peanut) oil
1 onion, finely chopped
1 garlic clove, crushed
5 ml/1 tsp ground turmeric
15 ml/1 tbsp mild curry paste
5 ml/1 tsp cumin seeds
15 ml/1 tbsp plain (all-purpose) flour
10 ml/2 tsp tomato purée (paste)

300 ml/½ pt/1¼ cups vegetable
  stock
Salt
250 g/9 oz block of firm tofu, cubed
4 eggs
15 ml/1 tbsp chopped fresh
  coriander (cilantro)

TO SERVE:
Naan breads and a green salad

1   Heat the oil in a pan, add the onion and garlic and fry, stirring, for 3 minutes until beginning to brown slightly.

2   Stir in the turmeric, curry paste and cumin seeds and fry for 1 minute.

3   Stir in the flour and tomato purée, then gradually blend in the stock and bring to the boil. Season to taste with salt.

4   Put the tofu in the crock pot and pour the sauce over. Cover and cook on Low for 2–3 hours.

5   Break the eggs into the curry. Cover and cook on Low for a further 20 minutes or until cooked to your liking. Sprinkle with the chopped coriander and serve with naan breads and a green salad.

Channa aloo is a delicious, filling and comforting curry that can be served on its own or with tandoori chicken or fish. I like to serve it as a main dish, topped with some wilted spinach and poached eggs. Use two large cans of chick peas and continue from step 3, if you prefer, adding the whole spices to the pot.

Chick pea and potato curry

SERVES 4

225 g/8 oz/1⅓ cups dried chick peas (garbanzos), soaked in cold water for several hours or overnight
2 cardamom pods, split
2 cloves
A piece of cinnamon stick
1 bay leaf
30 ml/2 tbsp groundnut (peanut) oil
2 large onions, chopped
1 large garlic clove, crushed
15 ml/1 tbsp pomegranate molasses
5 ml/1 tsp ground cumin
5 ml/1 tsp ground coriander
5 ml/1 tsp grated fresh root ginger
1 fat green chilli, seeded, if preferred, and chopped
1 green (bell) pepper, diced
15 ml/1 tbsp tomato purée (paste)
5 ml/1 tsp caster (superfine) sugar
Salt and freshly ground black pepper
2 large potatoes, peeled and cut into bite-sized chunks
2 spring onions (scallions), finely chopped, to garnish

1 Drain the soaked chick peas and place in a saucepan. Just cover with fresh cold water and add the cardamom pods, cloves, cinnamon and bay leaf. Bring to the boil and boil rapidly for 10 minutes.

2 Tip into the crock pot with the cooking water, cover and cook on High for 3–4 hours or Low for 6–8 hours until tender and most of the liquid has been absorbed.

3 Meanwhile, heat the oil in a pan, add the onions and fry for 2 minutes. Stir the remaining ingredients except the potatoes into the pan and add 150 ml/¼ pt/⅔ cup of water. Bring to the boil, then add to the chick peas with the potatoes. Stir, re-cover and cook on High for a further 2 hours or Low for a further 4 hours until everything is bathed in a rich sauce.

4 Taste and re-season if necessary. Sprinkle with the chopped spring onions and serve hot.

Slow-cooked pilafs have a slightly stickier texture than you may be used to – but they also have an intense flavour. To serve this for a dinner party, press a portion at a time of the cooked pilaf into an individual small dish and turn it out on to a warm serving plate. Surround the pilaf moulds with hot passata, flavoured with chilli and chopped fresh coriander.

Mushroom and pickled ginger pilaf

SERVES 4

350 g/12 oz/1½ cups basmati rice
30 ml/2 tbsp groundnut (peanut) oil
1 onion, chopped
1 garlic clove, crushed
10 ml/2 tsp chopped pickled ginger
5 ml/1 tsp garam masala
1.5 ml/¼ tsp hot chilli powder

225 g/8 oz mushrooms, quartered
900 ml/1½ pts/3¾ cups boiling
  vegetable or chicken stock
Salt and freshly ground black pepper
30 ml/2 tbsp chopped fresh parsley
  or coriander (cilantro)

1 Wash the rice well in a sieve (strainer) and drain thoroughly.

2 Heat the oil in a saucepan, add the onion and garlic and fry, stirring, for 3 minutes until lightly golden.

3 Add the ginger, garam masala, chilli powder and rice and stir until the rice is glistening. Tip into the crock pot.

4 Add the mushrooms, the boiling stock and a little salt and pepper. Stir well, cover and cook on Low for 2 hours until the rice is just tender and has absorbed the liquid.

5 Fluff up with a fork, taste and re-season, if necessary. Garnish with the parsley and serve hot.

This dhal is particularly tasty with the addition of the tomatoes. You can experiment using green or brown lentils too. Serve it with curries, of course, but it's also lovely just with naan breads for a light lunch. For non-veggies, it's is an ideal accompaniment to gammon steaks too! If you add more stock and purée it once cooked, you'll have an excellent soup.

Yellow split peas with fried onions and red chilli

SERVES 4

175 g/6 oz/1 cup yellow split peas, soaked in cold water for several hours or overnight
5 ml/1 tsp ground cumin
5 ml/1 tsp ground coriander
5 ml/1 tsp grated fresh root ginger
1.5 ml/¼ tsp ground turmeric
1.5 ml/¼ tsp crushed dried chillies
2 tomatoes, skinned and chopped
150 ml/¼ pt/⅔ cup boiling water
30 ml/2 tbsp groundnut (peanut) oil
2 large onions, halved and thinly sliced
2 fat red chillies, seeded, if preferred, and sliced
Salt and freshly ground black pepper

1   Drain the soaked split peas and place in the crock pot. Add the spices, tomatoes and boiling water. Cover and cook on High for 3 hours or Low for 6 hours until the peas are soft and the dhal is very moist.

2   Meanwhile, heat the oil in a frying pan, add the onions and fry, stirring, for 5 minutes until soft and golden. Add the chillies and fry for a further 30 seconds.

3   Season the dhal to taste, spoon into a serving dish and pile the onion and chilli mixture on top.

This is a robustly satisfying dish with loads of flavour. Try it served as below (perhaps with a green salad too) or spoon the mixture into crispy tacos, flour or corn tortillas or over rice for an even more substantial dish. You can ring the changes with different vegetables, too, such as broccoli for cauliflower or butternut squash instead of courgettes.

Chilli beans and vegetables

SERVES 4

100 g/4 oz/⅔ cup dried black eyed beans, soaked in cold water for several hours or overnight

100 g/4 oz/⅔ cup dried red kidney beans, soaked in cold water for several hours or overnight

30 ml/2 tbsp groundnut (peanut) oil

1 large onion, chopped

1 garlic clove, crushed

5–10 ml/1–2 tsp crushed dried chillies

5 ml/1 tsp ground cumin

2.5 ml/½ tsp ground cinnamon

15 ml/1 tbsp paprika

450 ml/¾ pt/2 cups passata (sieved tomatoes)

300 ml/½ pt/1¼ cups boiling water

15 ml/1 tbsp tomato purée (paste)

1 bay leaf

5 ml/1 tsp dried oregano

2 large carrots, diced

2 courgettes (zucchini), diced

100 g/4 oz mushrooms, quartered

½ small cauliflower, cut into small florets

Salt and freshly ground black pepper

TO SERVE:
Grated cheese and crusty bread

1 Drain the soaked beans and put in a saucepan. Just cover with water, bring to the boil and boil rapidly for 10 minutes to remove the toxins. Tip into the crock pot. Cover and cook on High for 2 hours or Low for 4 hours or until tender and most of the liquid has been absorbed.

2 Heat the oil in the rinsed-out saucepan. Add the onion and garlic and fry, stirring, for 2 minutes. Add the spices, passata, water, tomato purée and herbs. Bring to the boil, stirring.

3 Add the vegetables to the beans and pour in the tomato mixture. Stir well, season with salt and pepper, cover and cook on High for 2 hours or Low for 4 hours until everything is tender and bathed in sauce.

4 Taste and re-season if necessary. Discard the bay leaf and serve hot with grated cheese sprinkled over and crusty bread.

I've done various versions of this dish, shakshsuka, *before but this is my favourite. This lively mixture of spiced vegetables is perfect cooked in the slow cooker. If you prefer, use dried chick peas and cook them first (see page 115). To toast pine nuts, toss them in a non-stick pan over a moderate heat until they turn golden but keep an eye on them as they burn easily.*

Spiced Tunisian vegetables with chick peas

SERVES 4

30 ml/2 tbsp olive oil
1 onion, sliced
15 ml/1 tbsp harissa paste
1 aubergine (eggplant), sliced
1 red (bell) pepper, sliced
1 green pepper, sliced
2 courgettes (zucchini), sliced
1 garlic clove, crushed
400 g/14 oz/1 large can of chopped tomatoes
425 g/15 oz/1 large can of chick peas (garbanzos), drained

Salt and freshly ground black pepper
15 ml/1 tbsp tomato purée (paste)
150 ml/¼ pt/⅔ cup vegetable stock
50 g/2 oz/⅓ cup raisins
15 ml/1 tbsp clear honey
15 ml/1 tbsp chopped fresh parsley
15 ml/1 tbsp chopped fresh coriander (cilantro)
30 ml/2 tbsp toasted pine nuts to garnish

TO SERVE:
Flat breads

1 Heat the oil in a large saucepan, add the onion and fry, stirring, for 2 minutes. Add the harissa paste and fry for 30 seconds.

2 Add the aubergine, peppers, courgettes, garlic and tomatoes and stir to coat in the oil. Tip into the crock pot. Add the chick peas and some salt and pepper.

3 Blend the tomato purée in the saucepan with the stock, raisins and honey. Bring to the boil and add to the pot. Cover and cook on High for 2–3 hours or Low for 4–6 hours, stirring once, until the vegetables are cooked but still with some 'bite'.

4 Taste and re-season, if necessary. Sprinkle with the herbs and pine nuts and serve with flat breads.

If you come in from work and want this meal, but more quickly, use two drained 400 g/14 oz/large cans of red kidney beans and start the cooking at step 2. This will save several hours. The plus is it needs no attention at all in the slow cooker. It doesn't look all that attractive when cooking but, once dished up and garnished, it looks and tastes great.

Crushed kidney beans in creamy curry sauce

SERVES 4

225 g/8 oz/1⅓ cups dried red kidney beans, soaked in cold water for several hours or overnight
15 g/½ oz/1 tbsp ghee or butter
1 onion, finely chopped
1 cm/½ in piece of fresh root ginger, grated
1 garlic clove, crushed
15 ml/1 tbsp mild curry paste
10 ml/2 tsp cornflour (cornstarch)

Juice of ½ lemon
150 ml/¼ pt/⅔ cup crème fraîche
Salt
15 ml/1 tbsp chopped fresh mint
2.5 cm/1 in piece of cucumber, peeled and finely chopped

TO SERVE:
Basmati rice

1 Drain the soaked beans and place in a saucepan. Cover with water, bring to the boil and boil rapidly for 10 minutes to remove the toxins. Transfer to the crock pot. Cover and cook on High for 2–3 hours or Low for 4–6 hours until tender.

2 Drain off any remaining water, then roughly crush the beans, using a fork or potato masher, so they are slightly broken up but still chunky.

3 Melt the ghee or butter, add the onion and fry, stirring, for 2 minutes until softened and lightly golden. Stir into the crock pot with the ginger, garlic and curry paste.

4 Blend the cornflour with the lemon juice and stir into the crock pot with the crème fraîche. Season to taste with salt. Cover and cook on High for 1 hour or Low for 2 hours.

5 Taste and re-season, if necessary. Spoon the mixture over basmati rice and sprinkle with the chopped mint and cucumber.

This is yet another dish that's great topped with fried eggs – in true Mexican style! The amount of green chilli I've specified is quite a lot, but you can reduce it if you prefer. In Mexico, you'd add more than a dash of hot pepper sauce at the end, too, but that's in a country where they love chillies so much that they even use them to flavour strawberries!

Mexican rice with cheese and crushed guacamole

SERVES 4

350 g/12 oz/1½ cups long-grain rice
30 ml/2 tbsp groundnut (peanut) oil
1 onion, chopped
2 garlic cloves, crushed
3 thin green chillies, seeded if preferred, and finely chopped
900 ml/1½ pts/3¾ cups vegetable or chicken stock

Salt and freshly ground black pepper
100 g/4 oz/1 cup grated Manchego or Cheddar cheese

FOR THE GUACAMOLE :
2 ripe avocados
Juice of 1 lime

1 Wash the rice well in a sieve (strainer) and drain thoroughly.

2 Heat the oil in a pan, add the onion and garlic and fry, stirring, for 3 minutes until lightly golden.

3 Stir in the rice until glistening. Add the chillies, stock and some salt and pepper, bring to the boil, then tip into the crock pot. Cover and cook on Low for 2 hours or until the rice is just tender and has absorbed the liquid.

4 Stir, taste and adjust the seasoning if necessary. Top with the cheese, re-cover and cook for a further 10 minutes or until the cheese has melted.

5 Meanwhile, to make the guacamole, halve the avocados, remove the stones (pits) and scrape the flesh into a bowl. Roughly crush with the lime juice.

6 Pile the rice mixture on to warm plates, top each portion with a spoonful of the guacamole and serve straight away.

I love the combination of flavours in this dish. The lentils give it an almost meaty texture too. Okay, I've cheated this time and use commercial Madras paste instead of making my own but, if you prefer, you could use the home-made paste in the Madras Lamb Curry recipe on page 55 and add it at step 2 with the rest of the ingredients after you've fried the onion.

Aubergine, pea and lentil madras

SERVES 4

175 g/6 oz/1 cup green or brown
  lentils, rinsed
750 ml/1½ pints/3 cups boiling water
2 large waxy potatoes, scrubbed and
  diced
1 large aubergine (eggplant), diced
30 ml/2 tbsp groundnut (peanut) oil
1 large onion, chopped
1 garlic clove, crushed
45 ml/3 tbsp Madras curry paste

225 g/8 oz/2 cups frozen peas, just
  thawed
150 ml/¼ pt/⅔ cup plain yoghurt
Salt
30 ml/2 tbsp desiccated (shredded)
  coconut

TO SERVE:
Naan breads flavoured with garlic
  and coriander

1 Put the lentils in the crock pot and add the boiling water. Cover and cook on High for 2–3 hours or Low for 4–6 hours until tender and just a little liquid is left. Add the potatoes and aubergine.

2 Heat the oil in a pan, add the onion and garlic and fry, stirring, for 3 minutes until lightly browned. Stir in all the remaining ingredients except the coconut, seasoning to taste with salt. Bring to the boil and pour into the crock pot. Stir gently. Cover and cook on High for a further 2 hours or Low for 4 hours until everything is tender and just bathed in sauce.

3 Meanwhile, toast the coconut in a non-stick frying pan.

4 Taste and re-season the curry, if necessary. Spoon into bowls and sprinkle with the coconut. Serve with naan breads with garlic and coriander.

INDEX